HOW TO DO YOUR OWN
PAINTING AND WALLPAPERING

How to Do Your Own

PAINTING

and

WALLPAPERING

by Jackson Hand

Popular Science Publishing Co. Inc.   •   Harper & Row
A Times Mirror Subsidiary   New York, London

CONTENTS

Part I

INTERIOR
AND EXTERIOR PAINTING

INTRODUCTION

THIS BOOK has a well defined purpose: to help you keep your home looking its best. It is concerned mainly with the surfaces of things—walls, floors, ceilings inside and out—and with the materials you use to keep those surfaces new and pretty and modern. As we all know, a home can start to look old long before its time, unless a well planned program of upkeep goes into effect practically the day the house is built.

Not all of our intent in this book is cosmetic, however. Most of it is highly practical and has to do with value, with increasing livability and enjoyment, and even with the eventual *elimination of upkeep* to the greatest extent possible. Every year new materials come along that are prettier, more durable, easier to live with. Every year dozens of entirely new ideas take hold in the world of homes, and strike a new spark in pride of ownership.

Among major reasons why homeowners find it wise to keep on top of their painting, papering, paneling, tiling, and similar problems are the following . . .

First, the only way you can maintain your home at current market value—and it is an important investment, to be sure—is to keep its appearance tiptop. Real estate agents have told me that the first appearance of a house—the condition of its paint, the fresh look of its interiors—can make a difference of many thousands of dollars in the price the house would bring. Furthermore, the "clean" house, the "cream puff" as they call it sells faster no matter what market conditions are.

Naturally, few of us think of our homes as commodities, which we set out on display complete with price tags. But many of us like to keep up with the standards of the neighborhood, just in case . . . and as gestures of decency toward neighbors who may want to sell and will do better if all the houses on the street look good.

A second important reason for careful home care is physical protection. Although it is not within the scope of this book to cover actual home repairs, the protective value of proper painting is well known. Not only is the paint on the exterior of your house a defender against deterioration, but in such places as kitchens and bathrooms, the right paint can forestall expensive repairs indefinitely. For many years, in fact, the paint industry has said, "Save the surface and you save all."

The third most frequent reason for a strong upkeep and improvement program is the perpetual march of technical progress. Every year new

3

materials become available that are not only easy to handle, but are so much easier to maintain once they are in use that they make the career of householding more pleasant.

We have reached a point where few of us can find competent workmen to do the things we want done around the house...and perhaps even fewer of us can afford their fees. For that reason, totally aside from the enjoyment we get from taking the best care of what we own, most of us must be our own upkeep crew. This book helps with that work—makes it easier and more fun.

In the pages that follow, you'll find all you need to know to do a top job of papering, painting, and floor finishing. Under each of these classifications you'll find a careful evaluation of materials to help you with your buying. You'll find step-by-step instructions for each of the procedures you must undertake. And you'll find scores of detailed how-to tips gleaned from many years of working around the house plus many pleasant hours talking with homemakers who know their stuff and with the manufacturers of the tools and materials involved. Every idea, every material, every technique has been tested in the hands of nonprofessionals as a means of eliminating techniques which require long experience or special skills. You can be reasonably sure that what you see in this book you'll be able to do in actual practice.

CHAPTER ONE

NEW MATERIALS
MAKE HOME UPKEEP EASIER

ANYWHERE YOU look in today's home you see products developed in recent years that outdo their counterparts of only a short time ago. In their efforts to bring modern ideas for modern living to more and more people, manufacturers of everything you use from floor to ceiling and from family room to bath have improved their products. No matter what it is, it does what it is supposed to do better .... and it is easier to use and to maintain.

PAINT AND PAINT PRODUCTS. No doubt the best example of product improvement has been in paints and varnishes. When latex paints (water thinned, water clean-up) first came on the market, they made it much easier to paint a living-room wall. People took to such products as Sherwin-Williams Kem-Tone and Martin-Senour Spred Satin with such approval that the paint industry got the message. Everyone went into latex paints; then everyone started to improve and expand.

Latex paints have now come the full way. You can use them in such problem areas as baths and kitchens. DuPont came along with exterior trim paint and porch paint in latex formulas, and today you can paint just about anything with the work-saving, trouble-saving kind of paint that lets you wipe up spatters with a damp cloth and clean brushes or rollers with simple soapy water.

Today, with the introduction of latex enamels and latex primers—*even for metal*—you can paint every surface in and around your house with a high-quality, long-lasting latex paint product. Paint the lines on your tennis court, paint the swimming pool, the driveway, the basement floor, the lally columns in the basement. And wash the brushes in soapy water.

Meanwhile, new resins being used in clear finishes let you varnish a floor and watch it dry to a satin finish with none of that gauche glare—that wears and wears and would be insulted if you were to open a can of floorwax in the same room with it. (These same varnishes give you a rubbed finish look on fine furniture without rubbing.)

For those who want a high gloss finish, or for circumstances of extreme moisture exposure where they might be more appropriate, today's alkyd enamels build a better film than ever. Or—would you like to try the catalytic coatings considered suitable only for professional use a few years ago, now sold off the shelves of nearly any paint store in town?

NEW FLOOR OVER THE WEEKEND. We used to consider a floor a pretty permanent thing. Sadly, too, since so many of them were impossible to maintain. Nowadays people change the floor not only because they are tired of the old one, but because new flooring materials are so much easier to live with.

New plastic tiles and roll flooring wipe clean and never really need waxing, and that alone is reason enough for a change, not even thinking about the lovely stone, tile, brick, marble, and other patterns.

Parquet-style wood floors come ready-finished, in a thin form you can cement down the same as plastic tiles. Same with strips—all finished, uniform or random widths, complete with contrasting plugs. You can put a new floor in the living room in a weekend, ready to walk on instantly, beautiful to look at, easy to maintain. For real luxury, you can buy strips of walnut and other expensive woods embedded in vinyl, ready to go down with linoleum cement.

Genuine tile is no less simple to handle. Square tiles for walls, tiny tiles for floors both go in place with self-sticking mastic. The new grouts which go between the tiles are plastic—easier to use, less likely to crack and chip. You can find various shapes and patterns of small tiles bedded in a rubber mat. For floors or counter tops, you handle them just like foot-square tiles.

CHAPTER TWO

PAINTBRUSHES

Too MANY homeowners fail to recognize the importance of good painting tools. They buy a bargain-priced, make believe brush and expect to like the results it gives them. This is too bad. The tools of painting are as important as those of any other job. You can do better work faster with a good brush—the right brush for the type of work.

WHAT A GOOD BRUSH DOES FOR YOU. A good paintbrush works well the first time you use it—and it gets better with use, as its bristles work in and take shape. It flows paint on smoothly and evenly without digging up furrow-like bristle-marks that ruin your work. A cheap brush is incapable of laying on and brushing out a good coating of paint. As a result, you spend all of your time trying to produce smooth work with a tool that can't do the job. It's like trying to smooth a board with a plane that has nicks in the blade. The harder you try, the worse it gets.

Not only does the good brush smooth out the paint, but it carries more paint to the job. Bristles of the proper length and resilience, properly spaced, pick up the maximum amount of material—without dripping. This, more than any other factor, produces speed when you paint; you spend your time brushing—not dripping. And, because you handle a lot of paint smoothly, you can often do a perfect job in one coat with a good brush, when you'd need two with a bad one.

A good paintbrush puts paint where you want it. When the bristles are the right length and thickness in relation to the width of the brush, you can gently feed paint into a corner, cut a smooth line between wood and glass on a window, flow an even coating on the curved surfaces of moldings and carvings.

A good brush, well constructed with the top-grade bristles, is easier to clean. It lasts longer. It is a worthwhile investment. Many a homeowner has a $10 brush hanging up between jobs that he has owned for fifteen years—that he has painted the house with three or four times. It's still a good brush, because it was a good brush when he bought it. One reason why: its bristles were all fastened in securely.

HOW TO PICK A GOOD PAINTBRUSH. You can tell pretty much all you need to know about a paintbrush by examining it. Is the handle well-shaped and finished—not rough and carelessly made? Is the ferrule a good snug fit on the handle, well fastened with two or more pins to a side? Does the brush feel good in your hand?

7

To judge the paint-spreading ability of a brush, learn the feel of bristles that flex just enough—not scratchy-stiff or floppy-soft. Brush shown here, 5 inches wide with relatively short Tynex nylon bristles, is a strong favorite for use with the extra-thick "dripless" wall paints such as DuPont's Lucite.

The most difficult part of any painting project is handling trim—particularly windows. Here are three styles of "sash tools," intended for meticulous trim painting. Left to right: angled, round, and square. They are not expensive; try all three over a period of a job or two, and see which works best for you. While the angled model works best around window glass for most painters, it is not as effective on flat or shaped moldings and trim as the oval or flat. For that reason, you may end up with all three.

In many cases, you'll find brush handles made of plastic, ferrules made of stainless steel, and the use of other components of materials unaffected by water. These are usually good signs of thoughtful manufacture, since so many brushes these days are used in water-thinned latex materials. But, even if you plan to work with oil-based paints, these waterproof characteristics are good; they protect the brush when you clean it with soap and water—as you'll do if you care for your brushes properly.

Bristles. Most paintbrush bristles today are made of nylon, the material which has emerged as the best-performing replacement for hog bristles which were once almost universally used. Although there were some problems with performance when nylon first appeared in paintbrushes, they have been worked out, and nylon is equal or superior to natural bristles in every respect at a much lower cost to buy. However, cheap and shoddy brushes are still being made with nylon, and you should be able to tell the difference.

Bristle length. When bristles are too short, they are usually too stiff. Some makers of shoddy brushes overcome this by using a finer bristle. The brush turns out to be floppy as soon as it is thoroughly wetted with paint.

If you do a lot of your own painting and furniture finishing, you'll find use for most of the brushes shown here, sooner or later: (1) small and medium round sash tool intended mainly for trim, excellent for chair rungs and similar surfaces; (2) angled sash tool with round handle, very easy to use cutting around edges, such as window sash and muntins; (3) 2 top-quality sash tools, identical flat handles, one square, one angled; (4) 4-inch wall brush for inside or outside work, costs around $8, good for many years of homeowner use; (5) outside wall brush, okay for use on any wall in the hands of an experienced painter, intended mostly for use with water paints on masonry; (6) excellent-quality trim brush with beavertail handle; (7) 2-inch varnish or enamel brush for trim or furniture; (8) three varnish brushes that double in enamel for trim.

The limp, short bristles won't carry the paint where you want it when you work in corners or around trim. On the straightaway areas, you find your-self babying the brush, trying to smear paint on the surface with the sides of the bristles—not the tips.

It is a general rule of thumb that a paintbrush should have bristles about 50 percent longer than the width of the brush. That is, a 2-inch brush should have bristles about 3 inches long. Bigger brushes often break this rule without loss of quality. For instance, a four-inch brush can be a great painting tool with bristles only 4 inches long. At the other end of the scale, small brushes often have bristles longer than the rule. A 1-inch brush may have 2-inch bristles. Shorter bristles would be too stiff.

Flexibility. This quality, of course, relates to length. Bristles should bend like a fishing rod or like a fencing foil—more at the tip, less at the base. You can judge this quality by flexing the bristles with your fingers. Beware of a brush whose bristles bend at the base while the major length stays relatively straight. It can never lay on a smooth layer of paint.

Shape. The reason why hog bristles reigned supreme in the paintbrush industry for so long is their characteristic shape. Thicker at the base, hog bristles taper gently toward the tip, and at the exact end they break up into tiny fibrilations called "flags." This taper and tip are duplicated in the best nylon bristles. You can see it if you examine the bristle carefully. The fine, almost invisible flags give the smoothest possible application of the finish.

Beware of these. Nylon bristles that are very fine and silky soft as you feel them. Stubby nylon bristles with blunt ends, often so coarse they feel sharp against the palm of your hand. Short, squared-ended hog bristles which feel sharp. It is impossible to paint well with either the too-soft or the too-stubby bristles, nylon or "natural."

Most of the qualities of nylon brushes make them superior to bristle brushes for most homeowner uses. There are painters who stoutly insist that nylon will never replace bristles, but these are often the same persons who insist that latex paints would never amount to anything. Nylon bristles wear better, last longer, paint better, and clean more easily than bristle. Nylon bristles are ideal for—they are specified for—latex paints, which are now by far the most widely used paints. A good nylon brush may cost a third as much as a bristle brush capable of equal performance.

KINDS OF BRUSHES YOU NEED. You can do all the brushwork there is around a house with three brushes:

A wall brush. This is a man-size tool, ranging in width from 3 inches to 6 inches or more. The ideal size for most nonprofessionals is 4 inches. Most women find it easier to handle a 3-inch brush. The difference is great in weight and ease of handling, and it is not significant in painting speed.

If you spend enough for a good wall brush (something around $7 or so) you can paint the inside and the outside of your house with it for the rest of your life — provided you clean it promptly and well after each use.

A sash tool. This is the name given to narrower brushes used for fine work around windows and other tight places. There are three kinds: square, angled, and oval. They all do the job, and the only way you can tell which one you like best is to try them. Generally, the angled sash tool turns out to work best for most people. The reason for this is that when you use it with an edgewise stroke—as opposed to flat painting—the angle is just about equalized by the flexing of the bristles. Thus—although the brush is angled in construction, it is square in use.

Trim brush. This is a medium-sized brush—about 2 inches—which you use for areas too small for the wall brush, but not difficult enough for the sash tool. Since it is used largely for *enamel* (normally the choice for trim, doors, etc.) your choice might be a varnish brush; you could then use it interchangeably with varnish.

The trim brush is the one you use to go around edges as a companion to a roller, if you choose not to brush the big areas.

All of these brushes come in a variety of handle styles. Again, the choice is entirely personal. You buy the brush that feels best in your hand. A sash tool with a round handle is often most natural for most home-owners to use, since its shape is similar to a pencil or a pen, and it is always used for work delicate enough so that the similiarity is a convenience.

HOW TO MAKE A PAINTBRUSH LAST FOREVER. A paintbrush is pretty hard to wear out, since the only point of wear is the bristle tips—and they are usually well lubricated with paint. But it is easy to ruin a brush by not taking care of it. The greatest and most frequent offense is improper cleaning.

Clean a brush immediately after you finish using it. If you are involved in a project lasting more than one day, store the brushes overnight in the thinner for the paint. That is, store a latex paintbrush in water, an oil paintbrush in paint thinner. It is not necessary to *clean* the brushes. Merely suspend them in a container of the thinner, without agitation. Be sure

Clean brushes in the thinner intended for the paint you're using—or buy one of the several fast-working brush cleaners paint stores handle. Many of them are reusable, making the trick shown here feasible. Keep the cleaner in a wide-mouth jar with a screw-on cap, such as a peanut-butter jar, and you won't have to bother pouring it in and out of the bottle.

For overnight storage while an extensive job is in progress, rig your brushes this way. A hole through the handle of each brush takes a length of wire which holds all the brushes off the bottom of the coffee can. Fill the can with enough water or paint thinner (depending on material being used) to come up well over the bottom of the ferrule. Some professionals use a mixture of half turpentine, half linseed oil for such storage when they use oil paints.

that the water or the paint thinner covers all the bristles, reaching up above the edge of the ferrule. Be sure, also, that the bristles do not rest on the bottom of the container. A good way to do this is to drill a hole through the handle of the brush and hang it on a length of coat-hanger wire resting across the top of the container.

The object of this method of in-progress storage is to prevent the paint in the brush from hardening even the slightest amount. When you resume painting the next day, you merely shake out excess thinner and brush a few strokes on old newspaper to dry the bristles.

Another method of overnight storage—or storage for longer periods, if necessary, is with brush-preserving jellies available at paint stores. (One trade name is Stat.) These jellies coat the bristles *over the edge of the ferrule* and prevent the paint or enamel from drying. Return the brush to use by wiping the brush keeper off with old rags.

At the end of the job, follow these steps for a clean brush:

LATEX PAINT

1. Be sure to clean brushes as quickly after use as possible.

2. Rinse out most of the paint under a water faucet.

3. Mix a mild solution of dishwashing soap; detergents are not necessary and may actually make the job harder.

4. Thoroughly agitate the brush in the soap, making sure the solution works well up into the heel.

5. Rinse repeatedly in warm water until no more color shows.

6. Lift brush straight out of the water, so bristles are naturally straight. Hang the brush up dripping wet, to drain dry.

OIL PAINT

1. Use an inexpensive petroleum solvent such as kerosene, which is cheap enough so you can use plenty.

2. Agitate the brush in a relatively small quantity of this solvent, then pour it out.

3. Repeat this until no more than a trace of color remains.

4. Finally, switch to turpentine for final cleaning until no pigment remains. As an alternative, follow the kerosene rinse with thorough washing in soap and water until rinse shows no color.

5. Hang to dry. Avoid soaking natural bristle brushes in water for too long a time. Never use hot water on natural bristles.

There are excellent paintbrush cleaners on the market. Some painters prefer these cleaners (which can be liquid or powder) to cleanup with standard solvents or water. Try one of them sometime. It may suit your way of working.

Whatever method you use, be meticulous about cleaning the paint out of the heel of the brush. If necessary, use an old fork to probe and prod the paint loose. Without careful cleaning, the paint will gradually build up to a point where the effective length of the bristles is too short for good work.

Solvents for other finishes. From time to time you may use finishing materials other than paint and enamel. Clean a brush used in lacquer with lacquer thinner, or one of the multisolvent brush cleaners paint stores sell. If you use shellac or one of the pigmented shellac sealers, you'll be delighted at the ease of cleanup using ammonia.

CHAPTER THREE

ROLLERS AND APPLICATORS

MOST PAINTERS, amateur and professional, find that a roller gives them a faster and better job on walls, ceilings, and other relatively large surfaces than is possible with a brush. In addition, the gentle stipple-like texture a roller leaves on the surface is appealing to most observers. This has produced a booming market for paint rollers and has encouraged manufacturers to do some research into which rollers do which jobs best.

Meanwhile, a number of oddball applicators are now available, ranging from fuzzy mittens to plastic-foam pads, and some of these surprise you with their excellence in use.

The wide selection of rollers today has been made possible largely by the adoption by the roller makers of synthetic fibers such as Union Carbide's Dynel and DuPont's Orlon. Rayon is used too, for rollers which don't cost very much, but these don't perform very well, either, particularly with latex paints; the water makes the rayon too soft. Lambswool and mohair continue in use, but they are not recommended as highly for latex paints as the synthetics. (You may not be able to find rollers specifically labeled Dynel or Orlon, but in most cases the roller maker uses a trademark of his own which gives you a clue. Examples are Baker's Bak-o-Nel and EZPainter's Pronel.)

The advantage of the synthetic fibers is the way they maintain their resilience even when wet. This means the roller has the same paint-spreading characteristics at the end of the job as it had at the beginning. It means, too, that the roller will wash clean and the pile will stand up the way it did when it was new. You get many, many paintings out of a good roller cover made of good synthetic fibers.

HOW TO PICK A ROLLER. A paint roller is composed of a handle and a cover. You can save money on both—but it will cost you a lot of torment in the end. A good roller handle is engineered so that you can slip a cover on—and get it off easily. It lets the roller turn easily, so it won't smear, but not so easily that it spins and spatters paint. Many of the better handles these days utilize plastic for the grip—because water cleanup of latex paints soon ruins a wooden grip.

You'll find two basic styles among quality roller handles. One has a core of sheet metal over which the cover slips. The other is in the form of a cage—several metal rods. Cheaper rollers require the removal of wing-nuts when you change covers—a bothersome nuisance.

Of the slip-on styles, the slight favorite is the cage style, since covers are less likely to "freeze" on it than on the sheet-metal core.

14

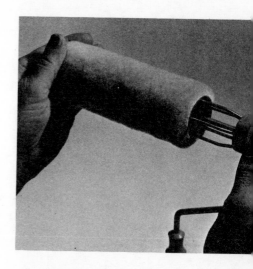

A paint roller worth having is composed of a good handle and a good cover. The cover slips on and off easily, so you can change your roller for various painting conditions. One of the best has a core composed of several steel rods which hold the cover firmly, yet release it easily without "freezing" on with dried paint.

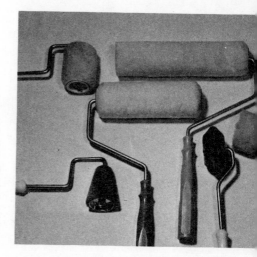

Representative roller shapes. The conical and V-shape rollers are intended for use in corners. The two narrow versions let you use the speed of rolling in small areas, such as between windows. You'll find a narrower roller works best on a severely uneven wall, where a longer roller would bridge low spots and leave gaps. Note the beveled ends of the two larger rollers. This helps avoid messy end fringe.

Range of roller cover types. From left to right are two carpet covers, used for texturing; foam cover many painters like for latex-enamels; three average-nap covers for most interior work; two long-nap covers intended for roughboard fences, masonry, chain-link fences, and other extremely rough situations.

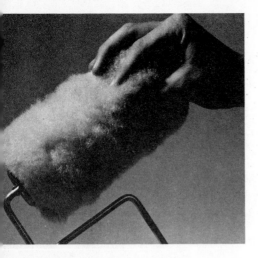

A roller works best when the cover has a resilient, springy nap with the fibers spaced for enough apart so paint can fill in between them and give you a fair amount of painting per load. You learn quickly how to feel the right resilience.

One of the biggest shortcomings of roller painting is a tendency to overspread. You can buy a special cover stamped with the reverse of the word "fill," so that the word prints on the wall when the paint load is used.

Good tool for painting curved surfaces—even pipes and columns—is a roller composed of several narrow units strung on a spring. It will conform to just about any outside curve.

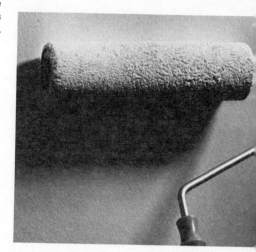

All the evidence you need that good covers are worth their cost is illustrated here. The synthetic fiber roller cover maintains its shape and texture, capable of laying on a good coat of paint. The cheap cover's nap flops every which way, leaves an uneven smear of paint, and many bubbles.

Constant-feed paint roller has a compressor and a means of locking a full gallon of paint into the line, so that its contents are pressured to the roller at just the rate for perfect painting.

Another feature of the handle to look for is provision for an extension, which screws into a threaded socket at the end.

You should spend somewhere in the neighborhood of $1.30 for a good handle—one that will last a long time. The 9-inch size runs about $1.50. If you want a really fine outfit, you can pick up a 9-inch cage style, heavy duty, for about $2.25.

Selecting a roller cover. The better roller covers are formed over tubes of plastic or screen or other material unaffected by moisture. Cheaper covers, on ordinary paper tubes, may soften during washing. Aside from these considerations, your primary concern selecting roller covers is the nap. . . .

Fiber length. Long nap rollers are for rough surfaces. Shorter nap lays on a smoother coating. This sets up a good rule of thumb:

Always use the shortest nap compatible with the job.

For most work you'll do, this means a ¼-inch pile. For rough plaster, masonry, blocks, and similar degrees of texturing, move up to ⅜-inch or longer. Very rough masonry might call for ¾-inch. They make rollers with nap as long as 1¼ inches, for such problems as chain-link fences, etc.

Fiber density. The density of the pile—i.e., the space between fibers— is an important factor in coverage and speed. If the fibers are too close together, there is no room among them for paint. If they are too far apart, they don't provide the capillary action to hold a full load of paint. It is not easy to appraise this quality. Laboratories do it by weighing a dry roller and comparing it with the weight of one loaded with paint. Your best bet is to spread the fibers with your fingers. If you can see through them to the base of the fabric, they are too sparse.

Fiber denier. This is the thickness of an individual fiber. You've heard the word in description of nylon stockings. You might prefer to use a word like "caliper." Denier is carefully balanced against fiber length, so that the roller will be neither too soft nor too stiff. Fibers must have enough spring to work into the low spots of a textured surface, yet not so much that they tip-scratch the paint they deposit.

Roller shape. A roller should be a reasonably perfect cylinder, of course. For most troublefree use, however, the ends should be slightly beveled. If they are not, the paint will gradually force the fibers at the ends into little frills which then overload and leave little dabs of paint which you must roll out—leaving more little dabs.

You can pay as little as 75 cents for *two* rayon rollers in an unmarked plastic bag. They may even have a long-nap look of luxury about them. But they won't paint. You end up blaming such innocent people as the manufacturer of the paint. Please don't.

Spend twice or more than that for one cover. Wash it—an easy job with latex paints—and use it many times. Cost becomes insignificant. You get a respectable job.

SPECIAL SHAPES AND SIZES. The basic paint roller for most uses is the 7-inch cylindrical model. You can paint faster with the 9-inch size, and there is no reason—no excessive weight or awkwardness—why you shouldn't use it exclusively for broad work. Some paint stores may also carry a jumbo-sized roller—one with a larger core and cover. The big ones are intended mainly for professionals but anyone can handle them. They pick up more paint and roll it farther than smaller rollers, for the simple reason that they offer more nap area.

You'll find a lot of usefulness in smaller rollers, and in some of the odd shapes. Look over the variously shaped rollers your dealer carries, to see if there isn't a work-saver for you among them. For instance, narrow rollers let you work in confined areas—as between windows. The one in the form of a truncated cone is good for corners and doubles as a crack-painter when you work on V-board paneling. A real work-saver in its specialized field is a roller with several individual "wheels" mounted on a spring, so that it will wrap around pipes or lally columns, cutting the time needed for such puttery work.

ACCESSORIES FOR ROLLER PAINTING. In addition to such staple items as the tray and the extension handles, there are several useful accessories to make roller painting faster and easier.

• A half-gallon reservoir with a plastic tray which screws on somewhat in the manner of a lid. When you tilt the outfit, paint comes up from the reservoir and recharges the tray. This is an obvious timesaver for painting anywhere, but it is most valuable when you are up a ladder and don't have to come down every time your tray runs dry.

• A plastic diamond-grid mat that clips on the regular tray, making it easier to roll out a fresh roller-load without the nuisance of skidding.

• A special steel grid designed to hang inside a 5-gallon paint pail

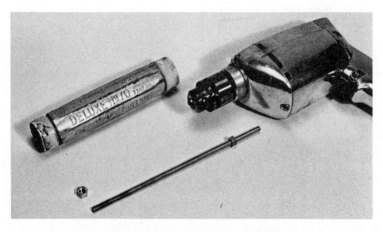

Cleaning a roller is easy with this improvised rig. It's a length of threaded rod, a couple of nuts, and the core from an old paint roller. Assembled, the outfit chucks into a quarter-inch drill. Slip the cover off the roller you are using and on this core for cleaning.

As you dunk the roller cover in a series of cleaning baths, spin the excess out. If you stick it in a paper bag, nobody gets sprayed.

and serve as a platform on which you roll off the surplus, the same as you do on the slanting surface of an ordinary tray. The accessory is aimed at the commercial market, but it is useful whenever you work with a material you might normally buy in 5-gallon cans. It more or less presupposes an extension handle, and suggests itself for such offbeat jobs as painting the garage floor, or the driveway, or the tennis court.

• Cleaning aids are available at most hardware stores. Most useful are a crescent-shaped, scraper-like tool used to squeegee the thinner or water from the roller, and a special spinner which whirls the roller at a high speed, throwing the cleaning liquid out by centrifugal force. This method of cleaning is fairly easy to duplicate using an electric hand drill and a modified roller handle.

HOW POWER-FEED PAINT ROLLERS WORK. One of the newest ideas in paint rollers is one that takes paint straight from the can, through a tube under air pressure. You can spread a whole gallon of paint without monkeying with a tray—without the need for reloading the roller every few seconds.

The outfit consists of a tube-handled roller, a length of neoprene tubing, a compressor, and a device for attaching the paint can. A control at the roller handle lets you adjust the speed of feed to match your own speed of rolling. There is a shut-off valve for times when you want to take a breather.

At first, this rig seems cumbersome. It is in the 9-inch size. The core is filled with paint at all times (it oozes out through perforations to load the nap) and this makes the roller rather heavy. The tube acts somewhat

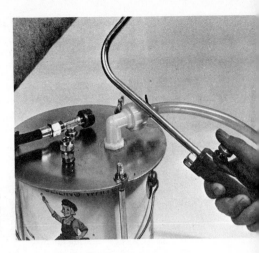

At the handle of the pressurized roller there is a thumb-valve. You can open and close it as you go—or adjust the flow to the desired rate and lock it open.

like a tether, restricting your movements. But—you get used to all this in a minute or two.

With it, you find that you are covering more surface faster than you ever painted in your life. You get better coverage, too, because you are not drawn by temptation to make individual loads of paint go as far as possible.

This pressure-feed roller is a big-job item, as you might guess. If you have only one wall or a small room to do, you might finish it about as fast—including cleanup—with an ordinary roller. Other disadvantages in-

Extension handle for the roller is a length of galvanized pipe, fitting the handle at one end, the roller at the other.

clude restriction to water-base paints unless you are ready to withstand the costs of the thinner needed for cleaning the rig when it is used in oil, plus the loss of a fairly substantial amount of paint that clings to the tube and the roller core, and goes down the drain during cleanup. You must figure on the waste of about a pint to a quart of paint every time you use the equipment.

Cleaning the tubes and roller are simple enough if you are using a

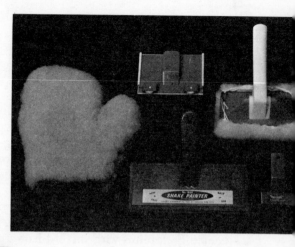

Typical range of "dauber" type paint spreaders. The mitten of lamb's wool puts paint anywhere you can hand-smear it. Center top is a short-pile spreader with guide-wheels intended to help cut a smooth line in corners, next to trim, etc. Top right is a handled version of the mitten spreader. The two rectangular daubers have short pile fabric cemented to a metal bed with handle. All of these unseemly gadgets spread paint efficiently.

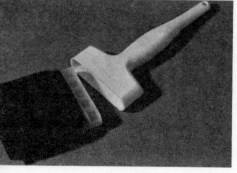

Snap-a-Brush is the latest nonbrush applicator to appear on the market. It comes in two sizes—3 inches and 1½ inches. When the job is finished, the "brush" is snapped out and slipped into a solvent-filled container, or discarded if worn. Instead of bristles, blocks of open-pore polyurethane carry the paint. A good feature: Foam tips don't become wider as normal painting pressure is applied.

latex paint. The neoprene tube has a standard hose fitting; you merely screw it on an outside faucet and let the water run.

(As this book went to press, the only announced manufacturer of the pressure-roller with national distribution was Thomas Industries, Sheboygan, Wisconsin.)

OTHER PAINT APPLICATORS. Most paint stores handle quite a collection of applicators for paint—many of them pretty unlikely looking, most of them surprisingly useful. The least likely looking—and most successful—of these are pads composed of very short, sparse synthetic pile, sometimes on a sponge backing, sometimes merely cemented to metal.

To use them, you dab them in the paint, then wipe them across the surface. They leave a great deal of paint on the wall—more than you could put on with a brush or roller. The results are no lap marks, little tendency to sag, and excellent speed. You can buy them in board-width sizes for siding or shingles, very small for sash work, even with little guides to help you work up close to inside corners such as the corner between wall and ceiling.

The semiscientific principle involved in these dauber-type applicators is the gentle vacuum created when you drag one smooth surface across another. The load of paint clinging to the substrate further contributes to this vacuum. Then, when the load is dissipated, the vacuum seems to break, the applicator lifts off the surface, and you dip again.

The applicators were generally designed for outdoor use, but you may have so much luck with them that you'll want to use them in the house, too. Replacement pads for the permanent handle are so cheap that they, not the bad-performing cheap roller cover, may be the answer if you are looking for throw-away painting devices.

CHAPTER FOUR

BEFORE YOU PAINT THE INTERIOR

GETTING READY to paint a room involves three operations. One of them is to clear the way so when you start painting, you are not held up by annoying interruptions. The second is to make sure the surfaces are in the right condition to accept a paint job without the chance that the new coating may not hold up. The third is to repair physical damage.

Clearing the way comes first, and in spite of the fact that it takes time, the net results is time saved.

To begin, if you are going to paint the walls, but not the ceiling, move all the furniture into the middle of the room, leaving traffic way along all the walls. If you will be painting the ceiling, move all the furniture into one corner of the room. Your procedure, when you start painting, will be to take care of the ceiling where you cleared the way, then put the furniture in the middle of the room, finish the ceiling, and take up the walls. In either case, it's a good idea to cover the furniture with a plastic drop cloth.

Take down all curtains and draperies. If they are candidates for cleaning or laundry, get that taken care of. If not lay them in another room.

Take down all pictures and other wall hangings. Most often, these will go back in the same places on the wall. If that is the case, do nothing about the hangers. But, if it is your intention to move or rearrange pictures and so forth, *pull the hangers* and patch the holes.

If there are electrical fixtures on the wall, unfasten the screws which hold them in place. Usually it will be okay to let them hang by their wires until you put them back. If there are any bare wires, turn off the electrical source and tape them.

Remove all switchplates and outlet plates—even though they are to be painted the same color as the walls. There is a sound reason for this: If you paint them in place, or "cut" close around them, paint may seep behind the plates. When it dries, they stick. Then, if some electrical defect makes it necessary to take the plates off, you may damage the plaster—making extra work at a time when you are not in a position to patch-and-paint easily. The best procedure is to spread the plates out on a newspaper and paint them separately. Don't forget the screws.

One of the blessings of today's latex paints is the way they do not show lapmarks. For that reason, it is often simple to remove plates, fixtures,

It is almost easier to unscrew ceiling and wall fixtures so you can paint back of them than it is to paint meticulously around them. Good technique is to lower fixtures, spot-paint behind them, then put them back when the paint is dry—assuming fast-dry latex materials. That way, you get all the monkey business out of the way, ready to set out full scale with your painting.

Remove all switch and outlet plates. Put the screws back so you won't lose them—and so you'll remember to paint them if you paint the plates. Lay out plates on newspaper and paint them separately.

etc., from the wall, spot-paint behind them, taking pains to feather the edges, then replace them when the paint is dry. When you go at the main job of painting, you do not have to spend tedious minutes cutting close to these obstacles. Meanwhile some of the turmoil of painting is reduced.

CONDITION OF WALLS. During the process of clearing away obstacles, examine carefully the surfaces to be painted, looking for unpaintable situations, as well as for physical damage.

Certain conditions are unsuitable "substrates" for paint:

Dirt. Excessive dirt of any kind, and any degree of oily-greasy dirt, must be removed. Paint won't stick to dirty walls, and dirt may cause discoloration or roughness.

It is not hard to wash a wall well enough for painting, if you go at it wholeheartedly. Get a big viscous sponge. Mix a pail full of warm water and a detergent. The basic ingredient of most detergents is *trisodium phosphate*. Most paint stores sell this chemical in powder form at low prices. You can use a product such as Soilax, or even a dishwasher detergent. This solution doesn't have to be particularly strong. Half a cup in a pail of water is usually plenty. (It is best to wear rubber gloves.)

Rinse as you go. Dry the wall with the sponge, so that little or no detergent remains when the water has evaporated.

Although it is not common, you may encounter some mildew on

indoor surfaces, particularly around window and door trim. Mildew looks like ugly gray dirt, but it is very difficult to wash off. The answer: household bleach, such as Clorox, which kills mildew quickly and removes the dirty look.

Old paint. Ninety-nine times out of a hundred, you paint over old paint. And most of those times, it's okay to go ahead and paint, if it's clean. But there are times when the old paint may mean trouble.

Calcimine, casein paint, and similar coatings (including whitewash) must be removed, because paint won't stick to them. Detergent, warm water, and a bristle brush do the trick.

Loose, scaling paint is usually the signal that something was wrong when the previous coat went on. Be sure all loose paint is removed. Scrape and sand into the surrounding areas; in other words, try to uncover as much of the trouble as possible before you paint.

Glossy paint is often a poor substrate—particularly if it happens to be a bit oily-dirty. You can clean it and cut the gloss at the same time with a saturated solution of trisodium phosphate, in very warm water. Dump the chemical into the water and stir. Add more powder until no more will dissolve. Then swab the solution on with an old paintbrush. Use a sponge to rinse and wipe. This operation takes off the shiny-smooth surface, leaving a "tooth" for the new paint to cling to.

Wallpaper. Latex paints go on perfectly over old wallpaper. You only have to worry about two things: is the paper stuck on tight, and is it smooth? If the paper is loose only in isolated areas, you may be able to lift it, apply wallpaper paste, and stick it on again. However, if there is general adhesion failure, the paper should come off. Paint dealers and wallpaper stores sell chemicals which quickly soften old paste, making removal a relatively fast and easy job. It is important to be sure all old paste is removed from the wall, since it would interfere with smoothness and with proper curing of the paint.

Sometimes wallpaper is too rough to provide a good surface for painting. This is most often true when the joints are lapped, for the extra thickness at the joints is conspicuous under the paint.

Although a good job of painting is possible over old wallpaper, most meticulous painters prefer to take it off. One of their reasons is the possibility that moisture intrusion might possibly loosen the paper at a later date—ruining the paint job.

Paneling. There is a growing trend toward paint for such traditionally "clear finish" walls as pine paneling and the like. If the paneling has finish on it, in good condition, no preparation is necessary beyond cleanliness. If you are painting bare pine paneling, guard against knots and pitchy areas bleeding through by priming with a material like BIN, a pigmented shellac which seals knots and pitch.

Masonry. Such surfaces as concrete or concrete blocks in basements or the brick fireplace you may have decided would look better painted or any other masonry are ready to paint if they are clean and dustfree. It is standard procedure with latex paints to spray masonry with water and let the moisture drain and penetrate until the surface is just damp. This helps prevent the porous material from absorbing the paint, thus saving materials and improving adhesion. The second coat over such areas should take paint normally. When the masonry is particularly absorbent, it is a good idea to apply a "masonry conditioner" as a first coat.

WHAT TO DO ABOUT PHYSICAL FAILURE. Most plaster walls tend to show cracks here and there, until the house has been up a few years and has settled into its final shape and size. Until this time, plaster patching is a standard part of painting routine—and it may continue in a minor degree for many years.

The job took a turn for the easier with the introduction of a vinyl-base patching or spackling material in ready-mixed paste form. This paste has excellent adhesion to plaster, wood, masonry, and other common materials, so it can be used for just about any patching job. It is particularly useful patching dissimilar materials—such as a crack between wood and plaster. Shrinkage is low, and two applications are not necessary except when the void being filled is in the range of a finger thickness. You can put latex paint over it as soon as the surface is dry.

Ordinary spackle or patching plaster may be preferred when damage is extensive, however, for economy reasons. Some plaster materials should

Experiment with various patching materials and you'll find some which suit you best for each kind of repair work your walls and ceilings may present. Bag of plaster of Paris is economical, as is boxed spackle. Water putty is excellent for small cracks and particularly patches involving two kinds of material, such as wood and plaster. Glazing compound is intended primarily for setting glass, but it is also a good patching material. Conversely, paste spackling putty is intended for cracks, but can be used for glazing. (Products shown are typical of several different brands your paint dealer may handle.)

not be painted until a curing period has passed, since they harden and cure, rather than merely dry. Read directions carefully, to avoid the possibility of paint peeling.

Very small, hairline cracks usually fill with paint, and require no patching. This is particularly true if you are using one of the popular thicker-bodied paints.

Cracks no wider than about an eighth of an inch require nothing more than application of the filler with a putty knife, if you are using one of the vinyl paste materials. Some careful craftsmen prefer to dampen the crack slightly with a paintbrush dipped in water if they are using regular patching plaster or spackle. This gives a better job, since the patch does not have its moisture drawn out by the absorption of dry plaster.

Larger cracks and areas that may have chipped away usually call for a physical bond, in addition to the normal adhesion of the patching material. The standard trick is to undercut the edges of the crack, forming a modified inverted V. When you impress the patching material into this V, it is keyed in place. When it hardens, it cannot come out without bringing firm plaster with it.

Most of the time, larger cracks must be filled in two stages. The first is almost sure to shrink—even with some of the patching mediums labeled nonshrinking. The trick is to level the first application, without smoothing it too much. Leave a rough or deliberately scarified surface for the second application to get a bite on. In extreme cases, you may find that a perfectly level patch will require three applications.

One of the problems you encounter patching an area big enough to be conspicuous is matching textures. When the surrounding plaster is smooth, you merely make the patch smooth with trowel or broad putty knife. However, when there is roughness to be matched, you may have to introduce sand. Also, you may have to match as best you can marks left by troweling the original plaster. With a little practice, you'll make discoveries on your own that will help you match textures. For instance, when you let patching material harden somewhat in a rough form, before you do the final troweling, you leave depressions very close in appearance to walls or ceilings deliberately texture-troweled.

One other factor in producing a close match is the way the patch will take paint. Usually you must prime the patch, and sometimes you'll need to spot-paint the area with one coat of the finish paint, to build up a matching paint smoothness.

Minor repairs on indoor trim are covered in Chapter 6, where trim painting is discussed in detail.

CHAPTER FIVE

HOW TO PAINT WALLS AND CEILINGS

ALTHOUGH THE proper order for painting a room is first ceilings, then trim, then walls, trim painting has been given a chapter of its own (Chapter 6) owing to the vast differences between it and wall painting. If your next job involves trim, flip a few pages to fill yourself in on shortcuts and tricks for making it easier to paint windows, doors, and woodwork.

FIRST, THE CEILING. The biggest painted area in any room is the ceiling, and it is hardest to paint, from both the physical and the technical standpoints. It goes best, however, when you approach it like a big job—with big tools and big ideas.

Use a big roller. The 9-inch size puts paint on lots faster than the 7-inchers. There is, moreover, a jumbo-sized roller, much appreciated by professionals, which is not only longer but bigger around, so it carries more paint. Not only should the roller be big, but the nap can be a little longer than you'd normally use. Again, the reason is to lift as much paint as possible from the tray to the ceiling with each reloading—without dripping or spattering.

Use a long handle. This lets you work from the floor, cuts down on the fatiguing business of climbing up and down to reach a ceiling which is usually just about a chair's height too far up for comfort. Some people find it difficult—or sloppy—to use the extension handle. If you are one, the alternative is a plank—a 2-by-12 is usually strong enough and wide enough for safety—and two sturdy chairs or a pair of stepladders. The length of the plank depends on the dimensions of the room, and 12 feet usually does the job. The best height, if you can manage it, is one that puts your head about 2 inches from the ceiling. This keeps your hair out of the paint, and requires a minimum of reaching up—which is tiring. The plank-and-chairs (or stepladders) setup, incidentally, works to save you time and work when you get around to the walls.

Before you can paint a ceiling, you must make a decision: what color should the picture molding or crown molding be? The answer is simple....

If the walls are painted, the molding at the ceiling should be the same color as the walls. If the walls are papered, or if your decor involves both papered and painted walls, the molding should be the color of the ceiling. However, if the room is trimmed in a color other than white—

Save time by using an extra-deep tray, if your dealer handles them. You spend less time refilling it. Since latex paints rinse off metal almost instantly, you can use a kitchen ladle to fill the tray, a big kitchen spoon for the fastest, most efficient stirring.

Even if you use a 7-inch roller, use a tray big enough for the 9-incher. This gives you a wider surface to roll out the paint, with the resulting smoother loading. And—the bigger tray holds more paint.

The edge of your painting along a wall should be at an angle with the leading edge at the top. Start each strip by cutting in the crown molding or plaster corner about 2 feet.

Carry a full roller of paint to the wall, and lay it on in a zig-zag pattern. Make the first stroke upward, to avoid paint running down the wall.

that is, if you are using an accent color from wallpaper, for instance—then the crown mold may be ceiling color or the same color as the trim, whichever you prefer.

Always paint a ceiling in strips across the shorter dimension of the room. By doing this, you can return more quickly to start the second and succeeding strips, and the chances of lapmarks are reduced.

First, use a sash brush or a 2-inch trim brush to cut along the edge of the ceiling and to paint the crown or picture mold *if* there is one, and *if* it is to be the same color as the ceiling. Some people like to cut all around the room at one time, then set to work uninterruptedly with the roller. Do it this way, if you like, although it makes more work, moving the scaffold or stepladder. It is more efficient to brush in the corner edges, then roll the 2-foot strip, brushing in as you go. When you come back for the second strip, brush in the edge—and at the end of the strip, take care of the edge there.

As was suggested in the preceding chapter, all your furniture has been moved into one end of the room. When you have progressed far enough with the ceiling job, move the furniture into the center of the room and finish the ceiling.

During all this, paint facing toward a window or a floodlight, so you can take advantage of the sheen of fresh paint to help you see how well you're covering. If you are painting with latex paint, you can always go back and touch up any skips or thin spots, but it's always best to inspect your work as you go, to eliminate the need to bring back tools and equipment for touchup.

TIPS TO SPEED PAINTING A WALL. The wall is clean. All the pictures and other hangings are down. Draperies and curtains are gone. Nail holes and cracks are patched clean and smooth. The furniture, in the center of the room, is out of the way.

Okay. Pick a corner—a right corner if you paint righthanded—a lefthand corner if you are a lefty. In the upper corner, start painting in an inverted triangle, about 3 feet along the top and about 4 feet down the corner. Cut in with the brush, then start with the roller and fill in the triangle. Back at the ceiling, extend the brush cut-in for another 2 feet or so, then work down the diagonal toward the corner. Keep this up until you have established a diagonal from ceiling to baseboard. Maintain this angle all the way around the room.

Why all the bother about the angle? Two reasons. With the leading edge of your painting on a slant back from the ceiling to the floor, you are always standing in front of unpainted wall, and if you should happen to lean against it, there's no harm done. In addition, if you should happen to drip on the wall below where the brush or roller is working, you drip on unpainted wall—you can see the blemish more easily—and you automatically correct it by feathering it out to avoid a thick blob.

As you come to windows, lead across the top and down the near edge,

Then smooth the zig-zag with horizontal strokes in both directions, and end up with light strokes from the new paint into the old, lifting the roller at the end of each stroke. Check for skips as you go.

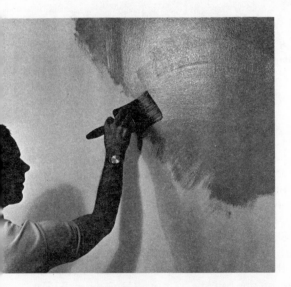

If you paint walls with a brush, follow the same on-the-angle practice, laying on, smoothing, then tipping off each brush load. Avoid uniform, same direction brush strokes or you may establish a texture pattern that is unpleasant.

then a little across the bottom. Back to the top, then back to the bottom, always maintaining the angle. This is particularly important if you happen to be using oil paints, since you must always get back to the edge while it is still wet, or lapmarks may show.

HOW TO MAKE A ROLLER WORK FOR YOU. Chapter 3 covered the selection of the right roller for the job, putting emphasis on the better performance you get from better rollers. To insure that performance, follow these steps:

1. Dampen the nap of the roller slightly, then roll it quite dry on a towel. This practice helps the roller pick up more paint more quickly,

To avoid any sign of lapmarks, tip off the load of paint finally with strokes that start in the clear and swing into the clear again before you lift the brush. This is the basic technique in "feathering" the edge of paint.

To avoid a dry edge—the basic cause of lapmarks—work part way across the top of windows, then part way across the bottom. Finish the top—then return to the bottom. And then resume the edge that angles back from top to baseboard.

and it also makes it easier to wash when you finish painting.

2. When you first load up the roller, run it back and forth several extra times on the slanting bed of the tray, to work the paint in well. Remember, the full load has paint not only on the tips of the nap, but between them as well. That way, there's a lot of paint—but no dripping. If you load the roller properly, you can paint two or three times as much wall or ceiling before you have to go back to the tray.

3. Spread the load of paint in a zig-zag pattern adjacent to the previously painted area. Be sure the first stroke is *upward;* otherwise, paint is almost sure to pile up ahead of the roller and run down the wall. For the first leg of the zig-zag, put very little pressure on the roller. Increase the pressure with each leg. That way, you apply the load about equally, and you use up all the paint the roller picked up.

4. Distribute the paint in the zig-zag with parallel strokes from the painted area into the bare, then with vertical strokes. Do not roll too fast. If you do, you may cause bubbles, and you may even cause the paint to fly from the roller in a fine spray, due to centrifugal force.

5. By now the roller should be fairly dry. Finish off the series of painting steps with light strokes from the unpainted area into the previously painted, lifting the roller at the end of each stroke. This way you finally smooth the job.

Reason why it is easiest to paint trim first, then walls, is shown here. Big wallbrush cuts close to trim, since it has the entire wall to rest on. If, on the other hand, you do trim last, you must cut along the narrow, precarious edge of the casings.

New latex semigloss enamels are tough enough for kitchens and baths—even shower stalls—giving you a complete range of water-washup paints for all interior painting.

When you work with small quantities of paint, pour them into an inexpensive paint pail, for easier, faster work.

Painting out of the original pail (or pouring out of it into a tray) fills the rim with paint. It will drain back into the can if you punch holes around the groove with a nail. This doesn't interfere with the seal when you recap the can; in fact, it makes it better since there is no paint buildup to interfere.

Most rollers establish a nap direction as soon as you start to use them. You get the smoothest job if you roll your finishing strokes in the direction of the nap. In the roller shown, this direction would be upward.

The ends of a roller may form a fringe which messes up the smoothness of your paint job. Clip it off with a pair of scissors.

Important: The nap on a decent roller always tends to lay over in one direction. If you roll with this lean, you get a smooth job. Roll against it and the nap tends to smear the paint. Look at the end of the roller to determine the direction of the nap. Then, by turning the roller over, you can always make a finishing stroke with the right lay of the nap, regardless of the direction of the stroke.

Things to avoid: Don't twist the roller while it is in contact with the wall, or you'll produce fan-shaped smears. Watch the end of the roller for excessive paint buildup, and when you see it, roll out the paint by running the end of the roller along the wall, held at an angle. Don't spread the paint too thin or you may turn an easy one-coat job into a difficult—and more costly—two-coat job. Remember the square feet of coverage mentioned on the can (usually about 450 to the gallon) is *an area you are not supposed to exceed,* never a goal you are trying to beat.

Always clean your roller (and other painting tools) immediately after use. Quick-drying latex paints are quick to set up on bristles or roller naps, as well as on the wall, and a roller which has stood around for half an hour or so is just that much harder to clean. The simple secret of roller washing is plenty of water. Begin by flushing away the majority of paint under the faucet. Then mix a mild solution of soap and water (don't use such strong detergents as dishwasher powder, Soilax, etc.) and dunk the roller thoroughly, letting the soapy water cut the paint. Rinse. Dunk again. Rinse. The roller is not clean until rinse water shows no color. The entire cleaning process is speeded up tremendously with a spinner. You can improvise one easily (see photo) and some paint stores sell them.

Lacking a spinner, you can whirl a roller fast enough to discharge final rinse water by running it very rapidly down any appropriate surface, lifting it at the end of the stroke. (You get sprayed a little, but it's just water.) Spinning leaves the nap standing fairly straight out. Hang the roller up to dry without disturbing the fibers.

What if you want to put a roller aside for a while—for instance, until after lunch? Lay it in a pan of clean, clear water deep enough to cover the nap entirely. *Do not agitate* the roller in the water. When you want to paint again, pick up the roller, let it drain, then roll it out on newspapers until it is dry enough to reload with paint. Another short-term storage trick is to wrap the roller snugly (no air spaces) in a plastic sheet, such as Handi-Wrap. Twist the ends, tightly, to keep out the air.

BEST WAYS TO USE A PAINTBRUSH. Although brushing is admittedly a slower way to paint than rolling, many homeowners like the textures a brush gives and find it easier to cover completely. If you have followed the recommendations in Chapter 2 on selecting the right brush, you'll get the best results with the following techniques.

1. Dampen with water the bristles of a brush to be used in latex paints, then shake and brush it dry on a towel or other cloth. If the paint is oil-base, dampen the bristles with turpentine. The purpose of this is to

Paint stores sell rollers in various odd shapes and sizes, many of them excellent specialist tools. This V-shaped model, for instance, is ideal in V-grooves of paneling.

Many painters find a plastic diamond-grid insert for the roller tray helps load the roller more uniformly, since it does not skid.

help the paint wet the bristles, and to make subsequent cleanup easy.

2. The first time you dip the brush, agitate it gently to work the paint in among the bristles.

3. Never dip a brush more than about half the length of the bristles. The reason for this is to avoid, insofar as possible, getting paint up into the heel, where it is extremely difficult to clean out. In addition, paint far up on the bristles doesn't come into contact with the surface in normal painting; it must be swabbed off in a way that takes time without putting much paint on the wall.

4. With modern latex paints, you can usually carry the full load to the wall without dripping if you simply lift the brush straight up, then

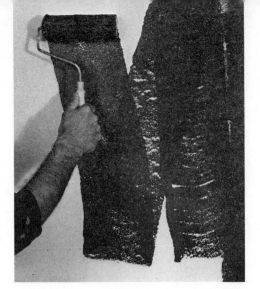

This is, in idealized form, the way you should lay on the load of paint from the tray. Make the first upward stroke with gentle pressure on the roller handle, increasing the pressure with each stroke until all the paint is deposited on the wall. Then smooth out the paint.

let the surplus drip for a second or two. With oil paints, which run and drip more easily, you can speed up the drain-off of the excess by slapping the bristles against the inside of the can. Many brush experts advise against drawing the bristles over the edge of the can or pail. This admonition was sound in the days of natural bristles, when the scraping action tended to curl the bristles. With a good tapered nylon bristle, this is unlikely to happen, and if you like to draw the brush gently over the edge of the container, go ahead.

5. The proper brushing technique is to lay the load on, then brush it out, and then tip it off. This has been for many years the standard and classic brush-painting procedure. As you read earlier in this chapter, you should always be painting on a diagonal back from the ceiling toward the floor. To do this with a brush, you must work in brush-load-size patches, from the top down.

Lay on. Apply the freshly dipped paint across the width of the patch, laying on with first one side of the brush, then the other.

Brush out. Now, using medium-pressure strokes which bend the bristles slightly, smooth out this paint over the area.

Tip off. Finally, using just the tips of the bristles and very little pressure, level the paint. At the end of each stroke, slowly lift the brush, so that the edges of the paint *both in the painted and the unpainted area* are feathered thin.

It is critical, of course, that the newly painted area joins the previously painted surfaces with a uniformity of coverage. Keep an eye on this space, for this is where skips, misses, and thin spots most often occur.

Among inexperienced painters, there is a considerable body of opinion that final brush strokes must be parallel, and usually horizontal. This is not true. The best-looking job results when you tip off with every-which-way strokes. Then, if any brushmarks show, they do not show in a pattern.

CHAPTER SIX

HOW TO PAINT INTERIOR TRIM

TRIM PAINTING involves considerations of appearance plus durability. For instance, the trim at the bottom of a stairway leading to upstairs bedrooms occupied by a houseful of kids is going to need washing far more often than the trim around the window in a library. You would lean toward a paint strong on washability. On the other hand, if you want the trim to "disappear," as is often the case in living rooms, you can use the same paint on trim as on the walls. Washability may not be as good, but color match is perfect. Here are the choices for use on trim. . . .

Wall paint. When washability is not overly important, and when a perfect match *is,* use wall paint on trim. It may not be the ideal choice around doorways and other traffic points. But it is the *only true matching color*. Many paint companies produce trim paint in the same colors as their wall paints, but the match depends not only on color, but also on texture and sheen. This is true both of latex and oil paints. In a vast majority of cases, the difference may be less than critical.

Satin enamel. Wall-matching enamels for trim are available from most manufacturers in "alkyd" oil-base formulas, and from many dealers in latex, as well. Major paint manufacturers make alkyd and latex available optionally. The choice between them is based on two factors:

Latex enamel is easier to use than alkyd, since you can wash it with water and clean brushes in soap and water.

Alkyd satin enamel is more washable, a little more reliable in serious water conditions. For example, if your windows have a tendency to frost up a lot in winter, causing an excessive moisture condition, you might get a little better service out of an alkyd enamel. However, paint failure in such situations is more often due to *shortcomings in application techniques* than to shortcomings of either latex or alkyd.

Glossy enamel. The only paint for trim which can be called really "waterproof" is glossy enamel. It has too much gloss for most purposes, but it earns its way in bathrooms, kitchens, laundries, and other places where high resistance to water is critical. It is, of course, the most washable of all the enamels. Glossy enamel is not always available in the same colors as wall paint, but you can arrive at a close match with some of the custom-color systems.

HOW TO GET TRIM READY TO PAINT. In some ways, preparing trim for failure-proof painting is more difficult than preparing walls and ceilings. Owing to the excellent washability of satin enamels, it is easy to wipe trim clean and ready to paint. However, trim paint is likely to be dirtier—by the very nature of its need; much more trim is intended to protect wall paint or paper from wear and tear, dirt and damage.

Cleanup with a detergent in water, followed by a rinse and wipe, takes most of the dirt off. *If any remains* chances are that its resistance to detergent means it is all the harder to paint over successfully. Try turpentine or paint thinner on a rag. If that fails, invest in a small can of Wil-Bond, a multisolvent containing a variety of chemicals, each intended to cut a different kind of hard-to-remove dirt. Wil-Bond and others comparable to it available at paint stores have the special advantage of removing the brittle-hardened surface of old enamel, making it ideal for repainting. This surface cutting feature is one of the reasons why experienced painters always use a multisolvent over old woodwork. Quite often, the old material is an alkyd enamel, a substrate over which adhesion may be poor, unless solvent cleaning is used.

Most physical damage to trim paint is caused by hard knocks or by water damage. Wherever there is heavy traffic, you'll find worn spots, chips, gouges. These must be filled. Wherever there are openings to the outdoors—windows, doors—you'll find failure due to moisture penetration.

Worn spots. Usually, when the paint wears through, on account of traffic and handling, the bare spot is smooth. All it needs is spot-priming, so that your subsequent painting will make it uniform in tone and texture. Don't extend the prime coat much beyond the edge of the worn spot, and be sure to feather it out to make the edge as thin as possible. (The recommended primers for various enamels varies somewhat from manufacturer to manufacturer. See Page 00 on Painting Bare Trim.)

Chips. When paint chips away, it leaves a sharp edge—in contrast to the smooth edge left when it wears away. Use fine sandpaper to smooth the edge, so that it will not show under new paint. Then proceed as with worn spots.

Gouges. Now and then, severe damage will actually tear, cut, or abrade part of the wood away. Fill the depression with a vinyl patch material or with water-mix putty, making the fill a little thicker than necessary. Then, sand the extra height away, using sandpaper over a sanding block.

What to do where water causes damage. Everyone has seen the most carefully selected paints deteriorate completely in situations where moisture is excessive—particularly moisture-vapor. Since the paints themselves are manufactured to be waterproof (or water *resistant,* a term used in some cases when actual waterproofness cannot be proven) what causes the trouble?

Water *behind* the paint causes the trouble.

Water gets into the wood through cracks, more or less permeates the wood, then seeks to escape, in the form of moisture-vapor pressure. This pressure is great enough to push the paint loose.

In other situations, the wood may have been wet inside, although dry on the surface when it was painted. Again, the water turned to moisture-vapor and created enough pressure to lift off the paint.

The answer to this problem is easy to state, but not always easy to achieve. Whenever possible eliminate the source of moisture. When you paint, make sure that the wood is truly dry. In areas of extreme trouble— such as a south or west window where there are condensation and frost, further complicated if the window is in a bathroom—some extreme measures are indicated. Wait three or four days *after any water contamination,* before you paint. A 100-watt bulb in a metal reflector, used as a heating-drying device, warms the wood enough to gently bake out moisture.

Priming or pre-paint treatment is a good safeguard. Such wood conditioners as WoodLife or Firzite or Pentox often cut down on water penetration and make an excellent paint base. A high-grade primer should always be used; never yield to the temptation to let enamel be its own primer in critical situations. Most enamel labels recommend a primer. If the enamel you buy doesn't, ask your dealer for a primer of a penetrating type, based on an alkyd resin—well known for its strong adhesive quality.

Take special care to cover all joints well. Be sure end grain is entirely sealed. Always let the primer and enamel cover an eighth of an inch or so of the glass when you paint windows.

Remember: the object is to paint only dry wood, and seal it up the best you can against moisture intrusion.

STEP BY STEP FOR FASTER TRIM WORK. Painting trim is relatively slow work. You can spend more time on it than it took to do the walls and ceiling of a typical room. There are procedures long recognized as time-savers, for both windows and doors, where you spend most of your time.

How to paint a window. The number of different surfaces, the way they meet, and the need for some of them to slide make painting a window far from a hit-or-miss proposition. There is a right way—and it is just about the only way.

1. Remove lifts and locks. Even if they are to be painted, it is easier to dip them, then screw them back on after they are dry than it is to paint them in place.

2. Raise the lower sash and lower the upper, to expose the inside edge of the upper meeting rail. Paint that inside edge, the top of the meeting rail, and an inch or two up the muntins (strips dividing the glass), if there are any. *This is the critical step.*

3. Now lower the bottom sash, but not all the way. Leave a quarter-inch or so between it and the window sill. Raise the upper sash, again not all the way, leaving a little clearance at the top. This exposes all remaining surfaces of upper and lower sash.

Remove all window hardware. It is easier to un-screw it, then screw it back on than it is to paint around it—most likely with the messy results shown here.

Be sure that all loose and scaling paint is re-moved. Use a scraper, then sand the hard edges of chipped areas so they will disappear under new enamel. If you expose bare wood, as in the case shown here, spot-prime with the primer rec-ommended by the manufacturer of the enamel you're using.

To be sure dust and dirt don't leave you with a rough job, get out the vacuum cleaner as the last step before you start to paint.

Lower the top sash and raise the lower, revealing the inner face of the meeting rail. Paint the meeting rail front and top. The bottom gets outside paint. Finally, paint up the muntins for an inch or two.

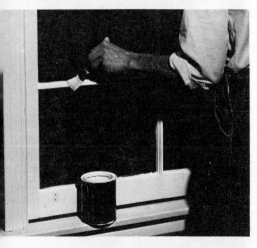

Paint the rest of the window. If you do it properly, you'll deliberately and carefully paint about an eighth of an inch of the glass, thus making sure you get a good watertight seal.

Following the muntins, do the frames, then the casing around the window, and the sill. Last, do the apron under the sill.

4. Continue by painting the muntins of the upper sash, then the frames. Move to the lower sash and do it, muntins first, then frames. Do not disturb the position of the window.

5. Next come the inner surfaces of the opening, followed by casings. It is standard practice to paint the grooves which the windows slide in *above* the lower sash (you get the groove *below* the upper sash when you paint outdoors), but it is not standard to paint the groove where it is covered when the window is closed. Painting this groove would contribute to a sticking window.

6. Finally, paint the sill and the apron below it.

When the window paint has dried, a gentle nudge with the heel of your hand will crack the paint which might cause it to stick. Run it up and down a few times, to be sure it's loose before you close it. If there is any doubt at all about the paint being dry, wait a day before you close the window, because once it is closed and paint-stuck, opening it is difficult —so difficult you could break the glass in the process.

It is tedious, picky work, painting windows, but decent appearance depends on patience. The most difficult part, of course, is painting next to the glass. Half the answer is a good brush—one that you can handle professionally. It may take a while for you to determine which size and which style works best, but you can learn a lot by handling several of them at your paint store. Sometimes it takes more than one style, and the price of two or three brushes is well worth the saving in time, when you consider that a good sash tool only runs $2 or less, and a good trim brush little more than that.

What you must learn to do is cut along the glass so carefully and precisely that you leave a tiny runner of paint *on the glass*. This is important, because it seals the vulnerable joint between wood and glazing compound or putty and glass.

How to paint a door. If your home has flush doors, the job is simple: paint them with a roller. For latex enamels, many people prefer a foam cover, although a relatively short nap Dynel or Orlon cover lays on enamel heavily enough so that it levels well.

Since it is not difficult to pull the hinge pins on doors that are hung in the usual manner, you can take doors down and lay them flat for easiest painting. This has the extra advantage on flush doors of permitting an extra thick application which levels and doesn't sag. Fast-dry latex paints make it possible to paint one side, turn the door over in an hour or so, and paint the other side. If you do this, it's safest to pad the supports with a couple of towels, since the paint is a little tender when it first dries.

There is little to be gained by taking down paneled doors to paint them, unless you happen to have adopted a color scheme involving two colors—such as stiles and cross members one color, panels another. When you do this, the entire stile and cross member must be painted one color, including the molded edges. Only the panel itself should be the second color. In another color scheme for paneled doors only, the moldings are

HOW TO PAINT A DOOR

Paint the panels of a door first, including the molding. Flush doors, of course, you paint just like any flat surface—even using a roller.

Follow with the cross members and stiles, then the edge, as shown here. The other edge should be the color of the other side of the door, if they are different.

Next paint the inside surfaces. The color continues to and includes the edge of the stop. The face of the stop and beyond is a different color in a two-color situation.

The door casing comes last. If you do trim first, you can be lax about getting trim paint on the walls, since the wall paint will cover it, and it is easier to cut smoothly along the wall than it is along the narrow edge of the trim.

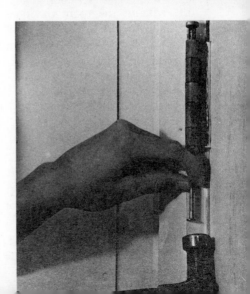

"Pull out" all inside corners of trim, to avoid overthick buildup and early failure. Do this by working the bristles into corner, as shown, then make the pull-out stroke slowly and smoothly, ending with the bristles lifted free of the surface.

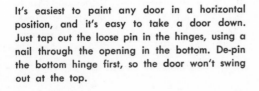

It's easiest to paint any door in a horizontal position, and it's easy to take a door down. Just tap out the loose pin in the hinges, using a nail through the opening in the bottom. De-pin the bottom hinge first, so the door won't swing out at the top.

the second color, with the panels and the faces of the stiles and cross members all the base color.

The advantage of pulling the hinge pins in two-color jobs is that you'll find it easier, always, to cut careful lines on the horizontal. Therefore, with the door demounted, you can lean it against some sort of support, then rotate it 90 degrees to keep the edges you are painting always horizontal and always on the bottom.

(Two-color work such as that mentioned here naturally suggests the use of masking tape. However, keep in mind that the tape will often lift paint that has not fully dried and hardened. This means you cannot take advantage of the fast-dry characteristics of modern paints. On the other hand, if you carefully cut the edges with a good brush, you can apply a second color as soon as the first is dry.)

The efficient way to paint a paneled door is from the center toward the edges much in the same manner as you paint a window.

1. Paint the panel or panels, including the moldings. Wipe off any paint which accidentally smears on the faces of the stiles and cross members, to avoid the chance of "fat edge" caused by extra paint buildup. Tip off the paint in the direction of the longest dimension of the panels. "Pull out" the corners—that it, generally work the bristles into the corners and make a final stroke which draws out any surplus of paint there, smoothing it on the panel. This brush stroke ends in the air, so as to leave no brushmark.

2. Paint top of the door and the upper cross member, feathering beyond its ends on the stiles, with horizontal strokes.

3. With vertical strokes, paint the stiles. Make one brush stroke run right at the joint between cross member and stile, so that you end up with crosswise strokes on the cross member ending precisely at the stile— and vertical strokes on the stile. Paint down on both stiles as far as the next cross member.

4. Do this cross member the same as above and butt past it on the stiles.

5. Finish the door proper by painting the edges.

Important: The latch edge of a door should be the same color as the trim of the room the door swings *into,* if the color happens to be different on the two sides of the door. This might be the case, for instance, when a hallway is one color and bedrooms off it other colors. The hinge edge of the door should be the color of the room the door swings *out* of. The reason for this is the best appearance when the door stands open; closed, of course, it makes no difference.

6. Next paint the inner surfaces of the door opening. Again there is a preferred procedure if the trim is not the same color on both sides of the opening. The color of the trim in the room into which the door swings should be carried to the door stop, *including the face of the stop against which the door strikes when it is closed.* The rest of the inner surfaces should be the color of the other room.

7. With the inside of the opening painted, move to the casing around

Good trick for painting shelves: cut the handle off a brush, so it is short enough to work back and forth in confined spaces.

Small paint daubers, composed of short pile cemented to a metal or plastic back, are handy for painting windows. You can keep them filled by picking up paint off a stirring stick.

the opening. At the edge of the casing, you meet the wall proper. Cut along this meeting line carefully, making sure that you cover all of the trim. If a little trim paint slops over on the wall, you needn't worry about it if you are painting trim first, walls last. The wall paint will cover as you bring it up to the edge of the trim.

Baseboards and other types of trim present no problems, except the need for cutting a sharp line along the shoe mold where it meets the floor. Many painters use masking tape on the floor to make this job easier, a particularly time-saving idea if you are putting on more than one coat.

WHAT TO DO ABOUT UNPAINTED TRIM. Since more painting done by the homeowner is over existing paint, most paint can labels are explicit in their instructions for this kind of work. However, they leave much ground uncovered when they tell how to use trim paint on bare wood. Although bare wood calls for just one additional operation—priming —there are a few precautions you can count on to give you a longer lasting job.

Preparation. Be sure the wood is smooth and clean. A wipe-down with turpentine on a rag after sanding is sure to help with adhesion of the primer coat—and *adhesion of the primer coat is essential.* Almost anything will stick to the primer, if only the primer will stick to the wood. When you work around the windows, or in kitchens and baths where moisture is bound to be a problem, an extra safeguard is a product such as Cleane-Woode, one of the multisolvents which wipe away almost any kind of dirt and contamination. Be sure the surface is dry.

Primer. The label of your trim paint will recommend a specific primer, intended for use with that paint. You can't do better than to use it. Some manufacturers recommend a latex primer for use under their latex enamel. Others forego the joys of latex materials insofar as primers are concerned and ask for an oil-base enamel undercoater. Generally speaking, in difficult adhesion situations (windows, etc.) the extra adhesion and penetration of alkyd-type undercoaters make them superior. You can ask your paint dealer for the oil-base primer for use under enamel that is recommended by the manufacturer of your trim enamel.

Remember, the purpose of the enamel undercoater is not just to give the bare wood some color. Its job is much more complex. It must seal the wood, so topcoatings do not soak in unduly. It must *adhere.* It must present a perfect substrate for topcoating, without the problem of sagging. That is why you must not use just any old paint as a primer—and it is why the enamel itself is never its own best primer.

Patching and filling. The best time to fill nail holes, cracks, etc., in trim is after the prime coat is dry. This keeps the solvents of the patching material from soaking into the wood.

Topcoating. One coat of a good enamel will cover, brushed carefully over a recommended primer. You'll like the results better, however, if you put on two coats. It will look richer, smoother, more professional. And it will last longer.

HOW TO WORK WITH TRIM ENAMEL. There is far more variation in handling techniques between various brands of enamel than there is between various wall paints. Some are thick and sticky. Some are thin and slippery. Some reveal their coverage only after they are dry (this is called dry hide). That is why you must do a little experimenting with the enamel you choose. Here are guidelines:

• Do not overspread. The latex enamels, in particular, are slippery under the brush, and many inexperienced painters put them on too thin. The latex materials do not tend to sag when they are applied in a full coating. On the other hand, oil-base enamels are stickier, and this leads to possible overapplication and sags and runs. When you work with alkyd enamel, you must constantly check back over your work, to be sure sags have not started, for they often appear after you think none are likely. When you find them, feather the sag out with brush strokes every which way, over a large enough area to redistribute the enamel in a safe thickness.

● Use slow brush strokes. If you brush too rapidly, you produce little skips where the enamel literally did not have time to reach into minute depressions. Slow brushing lets the bristles force the paint into contact with the surface, and insures better coverage *with less brushing*.

● Perfect the three-stage application technique: lay on, brush out, tip off—always recommended for application of paints and enamels. As you tip off, make the final stroke into previously painted area, and gently lift your brush as the stroke ends. This is the only way you can avoid leaving brushmarks.

● Be particularly careful when you paint in the danger areas such as windows, kitchen and bathroom sink and lavatory moldings.

● Remember that two normal coats are always better than one over-loaded coat—they dry harder, they are more resistant to wear, chipping, and moisture penetration.

CHAPTER SEVEN

HOW TO FINISH
AND REFINISH FLOORS

MANY HOMEOWNERS who gladly tackle the job of painting walls and ceilings, papering a bedroom, or even doing a whole outside paint project, shy away from floors. It looks too hard. Big, clumsy equipment. The huge area. All that furniture to move.

Those who have tried it agree, however, that floor finishing is one of the easiest jobs of all. The simple trick is this: since it is a big job, since it is a lot of area, just *tackle it like a big job* and it goes easy.

WHEN A FLOOR NEEDS REFINISHING. Let's start with an old floor that needs to be redone. First, there are some decisions to be made—some questions to answer. . . .

Does the floor need to be refinished completely, or is there a chance you might be able to put it back in shape by renewing it? Sometimes a floor that looks bad is actually only dirty. During many years of waxing and inadequate cleaning, the floor has accumulated an opaque overlayer that obscures the finish. This can often be cleaned away, and the finish beneath it may be sound.

Is the finish starting to wear off? If you can detect the beginnings of wear, you can often clean the floor carefully and topcoat it, without removing the finish.

Are spots worn through? If there are bare spots in doorways, halls, and other traffic points, it is sometimes possible to touch them up invisibly. However, sometimes you can't do less than the entire floor, on account of problems in matching the color and texture of the old finish.

Is the old finish overage? If the finish has been on the floor a long time, there is a chance that the old finish material is deteriorated, brittle, and not worth saving. You can check this by drawing the edge of a coin across the old floor in an inconspicuous spot. If the coin flakes, chips, and scrapes away the finish, it is a sign that it should be removed for a complete refinishing job. Any attempt to overcoat it will be unsuccessful in the long run.

Sometimes the effect you want—the modernizing touch—may not be available through refinishing of any kind. For instance, the very thing you want may be block flooring, instead of ordinary boards. Or planks. What if your floor is truly in bad shape? What if it is not worth refinishing? Check with your building supply dealer and you'll find there is a wide range of thinner-than-usual flooring materials intended to go down over existing floors with a minimum of cost and work. Since such overlay floorings are usually factory-finished, the job of putting them down is easier than you'd think.

CLEANING THE OLD FLOOR. No doubt you have often heard the admonition, "Never put water on a wood floor." Enough people believe this old wive's tale so that the world is full of dirty floors. Water can't hurt a floor that is *well finished,* unless you flood it with hot water and let it stand for a long time. It never hurts a floor to keep it clean.

Therefore, the first stage in renewing a floor that may not actually need refinishing is to *get it clean.* Get the accumulation of wax and dirt off. Expose the sound finish—if there is any—and see if it needs to be removed. There are two ways to get a floor clean:

1. Turpentine or paint thinner, used as a solvent cleaner, will soften and remove old wax. Using them, however, is a *fire hazard.* Be sure that there is no open flame nearby. Do not smoke. Extinguish pilot lights. Flood the surface with turpentine. Let it stand for a while to soften the wax and dirt. Speed up the process with medium-grade steel wool. Then wipe up all the dirty solvent. Finish by damp-mopping with turpentine or thinner on clean rags.

When the floor has dried, you'll learn a lot. Bare spots will show up. So will discoloration of the old finish. There may be areas or spots that are still dirty, for certain substances (such as sugar) are not softened and lifted by turpentine and thinner. You may have to go at such spots with soap and water.

2. Hot water and a detergent will clean an old floor right down to the remaining sound finish—and there is no danger of fire. Into a pail of water, mix a cup or more of a cleaning powder such as Soilax or trisodium phosphate, which you can buy from your paint dealer. The water should be warm—warmer than you can comfortably put your hand in. Mop the floor thoroughly with this solution. Combine the mopping with some serious scrubbing. Dry as you go. Then rinse out the mop and go over the floor with clean water as a rinse. If the rinse water shows much dirt, change it from time to time. Let the floor dry.

Now you can examine the floor, to see what kind of shape it is in. If it is sound, all over, all you have to do is put on another coat of varnish and you have a new floor. In fact, if in your opinion the cleaned floor is actually in top condition, all it may need is an application of paste wax, polished with a buffer.

If your scrubbing job leaves a floor that has bare spots here and there, you may have to remove the entire finish after all . . . but you may not. Experiment a little, to find out. Hand-sand a small bare spot and dust it. Then dampen a rag with turpentine and wipe it over an area that includes both the old finish and the bare wood. If the color of the wood and the old finish under turpentine is the same, chances are that you can revarnish and get no color variation.

In any spot-finishing situation after a scrubbing, you will find that the bare wood has been roughened somewhat by the water. This is called "grain raising." You can feel "whiskers" and slight undulations coinciding with the pattern. To sand these areas smooth, start with a coarse paper to cut down the high spots. Switch to medium, then to fine. The easy way to sand: Wrap two thicknesses of an old turkish towel around a brick, and use it as a sanding block. The weight of the brick helps with the downward pressure, and it saves a lot of work.

Whenever you find relatively large or numerous areas of bare wood after you clean with water or thinner, you probably will be better off to sand the entire floor and start from scratch. By so doing, you'll eliminate the chance of mismatched colors and the chance that waxes may have penetrated the bare wood, and would prevent the new finish from hardening. Actually, hand-sanding and spot-finishing many bare spots take more time than the big-job approach to the entire floor.

How to use floor renovator. Most professionals take a different route, cleaning and renewing an old floor. They use a product such as Dura Seal Renovator, made by Pines-International Chemical Company, Chicago. The renovator is, in effect, a penetrating floor finish with modifications to make it a floor cleaner, too. You might find it more to your liking than methods covered above.

Using the renovator, you work in patches and strips you can reach conveniently. With a big brush, flood the area with renovator. Let it stand about five minutes—but not over ten. Scrub the area thoroughly with medium steel wool wrapped around a brick. Now wipe the renovated area dry with rags. Continue in patches or strips until the entire floor has been covered. In many cases, the renovation is the whole job. You can wax it, if you wish, but waxing is not necessary. The renovator leaves a low sheen. If you happen to prefer a more shiny floor, let the renovator dry overnight, then use varnish as a topcoat.

Although the renovator technique was developed specifically for floors previously finished with penetrating floor finishes, it works well with varnish, although it is not recommended for shellac.

Remember, the best way to save work on floors is to avoid letting the finish get so dirty that cleaning it becomes a chore. Do not wax repeatedly without occasionally removing the buildup of wax products. Do not count on products intended for cleaning and waxing in one operation to keep floors clean forever. Now and then you've got to *wash* them.

Most important—never let a floor finish wear through to the bare wood. Keep an eye on traffic areas. When they start to show much wear (usually easily recognized because the wear changes the light reflectance of the surface), put another coat of finish on the wearing areas, or on the entire floor. Sometimes, depending on methods and materials, merely coating the worn spots will leave edges that show.

The difference between the new and the old finish will be inconspicuous—even invisible—if you carry the overcoat to adjacent walls, to the edge of floor covering, or other natural break-off points, such as the edges of boards. It is always best to spot-finish worn places, then put a coat over the whole floor.

HOW TO GET THE OLD FINISH OFF A FLOOR. You can remove an old floor finish two ways. One of them is with a regular paint remover or a water-based remover (Schalk's XX), a method recommended only in areas that are too small to get into efficiently with other methods. For instance, a small closet wouldn't give you room for sanding, and hallways *with the boards crosswise* would force you to stand across the grain, always to be avoided when possible.

Solvent-type paint removers leave you with a surface ready for new finish after only light sanding, if any. Water-mix removers tend to raise the grain of the wood, and you may find it necessary to machine-sand to produce the required flatness.

In the vast majority of cases, the efficient way to get an old finish off a floor is with a floor sander. Many paint dealers, lumberyards, and rental outfits have sanders available for a few dollars a day—and in a day they will take off a lot of old finish. Actually, you need two sanders: the big drum type for the major work, plus a smaller disc sander for edges and corners that you can't get into with the larger machine. If you happen to have a home-shop-size sander, you'll find it handy for edges, too.

The reasons for sanding are so compelling as to overcome any reservations you may have about using a sander. Professionals makes these points:

• Sanding removes a slight amount of surface wood—enough to make the color uniform, and to insure that any penetration of old wax will be removed.

Important: For this very reason, if you happen to be working on floors which are very old and owe a share of their beauty and charm to the normal coloration of aged wood, you must not sand, or you'll surely take off the color that years put on the wood.

• Sanding levels the floor, if it should happen that warping, cupping, uneven shrinking and swelling, or other idiosyncrasies of wood have left you with an irregular surface.

• Sanding gives you a virgin surface to finish—one compatible with any material you may choose, without the danger that an old surface may contain contaminants for a new finish.

Floor sanding techniques. The typical floor sander is big and heavy, but it is engineered in such a way that you don't have to work very hard to handle it. The sanding drum or belt rotates in a direction which would normally drive the machine forward. However, you hold it back. Thus, the action is one of a slow forward shuffle, as you lean slightly backward against the drive of the drum. You can adjust the amount of "bite," which determines the speed of sanding and the amount of forward drive. You soon discover that the degree of forward drive you can comfortably handle is also about the right amount of cut for a good sanding job.

The basic tool in floor refinishing is a heavy, high-powered drum sander (sometimes belt sander) which takes a tough and rough abrasive. Quite capable of sanding 1/16 inch or so off the floor, it takes you down to clean, fresh wood.

For confined areas and to handle edges where the cumbersome drum machine can't reach, a heavy-duty disk sander takes over. You can do some of this work with a workshop-type sander, but it is slow — and hard on the sander. Both the professional drum sander and the big disk model are easy to use, easy to rent.

In addition to the drum, the sander has idler wheels, positioned beneath the machine so that it rocks back, raising the drum off the floor unless a little lift is applied to the handle. Some models have an adjustable castered wheel in back; you can adjust it for amount of bite. Others depend on the amount of lift you apply to the handle. Either way, you quickly learn how to handle a sander, and your initial learning period, fortunately, is with coarse sandpaper, making the first passes over the floor. Subsequent passes, as you do the final smoothing, benefit from your accumulated experience.

One thing you must never do: never hold the sander stationary with the moving drum in contact with the floor. If you do, you'll grind a depression in the wood which is extremely difficult to sand out.

The three-pass system. One of the best floor-smoothing techniques involves diagonal sanding. It is called the three-pass system, and it goes like this:

1. Using No. 1 (50-grit) paper, cover the entire floor at a 45-degree angle to the floorboards. Work as close to the walls as you can, although you'll inevitably leave a sawtooth of unsanded floor all the way around. You take care of this later.

2. Switch to No. 1/2 (60-grit) paper and go over the floor at right angles to the first pass. At the end of this pass, you should have very little or no old finish or coloration left on the floor. By making these two diagonal passes, you get the maximum cutting speed from the paper, and you eliminate any cupping or warping of the floorboards.

3. For the third pass (which actually may be two or three trips over the floor) work parallel to the boards. Use 1/0 (80-grit) paper if the floor still needs to be cleaned up a little—not only smoothed. If the color is uniform, use 2/0 (100-grit) paper. At this point, the floor should be pretty smooth, but if you want an even nicer job, make a final pass with No. 3/0 (120-grit) paper.

The three-pass system as it is described above assumes floors are in pretty bad shape. If the floor you are working on is not discolored, needs only to have a poor finish removed, and does not show warping and cupping to be corrected, you can usually save time by making two passes *with the grain,* using only the No. 1/2 paper for the first and the No. 2 for the second. It is a good idea to make these two passes facing in opposite directions.

Parquet or block flooring. When a floor is laid in blocks with alternating grain direction, it is impossible to sand without covering half the blocks cross-grain. After you have finished the diagonal sanding on such floors, switch to the long dimension of the room and make at least two passes, finishing up with the finest paper you can obtain. The fine paper does produce cross-grain scratches, but they are so small that the floor looks good, regardless. (Now and then you run into a block floor laid diagonally; when you do, make your first two passes parallel to the wall, your final sanding parallel to the joints between the blocks.)

Important: When a floor has a heavy load of old finish, the sandpaper is quickly filled with an accumulation of dust and finish resins. This makes it useless. To get more life out of the paper, buy a variety called open coat, which has a great deal of space between particles of grit, and does not load up so quickly. Do not, however, use open-coat papers for your finer sanding, after the finish has been removed. If you do, you may put scratches in the wood which you'll have trouble sanding out.

Sanding the edges of the floor. By working as close to the side walls as possible with the big sander, you can eliminate a lot of edging work. Most

STEP BY STEP METHOD OF FLOOR FINISHING

1. Remove furniture, rugs, drapes, curtains, and any other conveniently moved equipment.

2. Remove foot molding and number each piece. Countersink floor nails below surface.

3. Rough sanding with drum machine removes coatings from broad areas. Use coarse sandpaper. Flex ends to ease entry into drum. First, sand floor diagonal to boards. Begin near corner, lower drum gently at start, and raise smoothly at end of each path. Go forward and backward over each path. Overlap paths a few inches. Next, sand floor in opposite diagonals like an "X". Then do 3rd sanding parallel to boards.

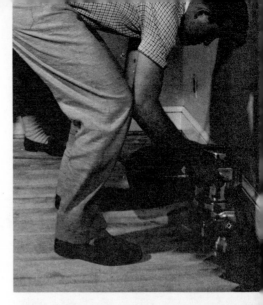

4. Rough sanding with edger machine removes old coatings from borders, closets, stairs. Use coarse sandpaper. Edger does most areas not reached by drum sander. Check light bulb at front. Start near corner against baseboard, working outward to blend with edges of broad areas. With feet about 2 feet apart, roll edger parallel with wall, doing about 18-inch sections at a time. Rest occasionally.

5. Preparatory sanding with drum machine gets broad areas ready for finish sanding. Use medium-grit sandpaper. This is first stage in finishing new floors or second stage in refinishing old floors. If new floors, first sand diagonally, then parallel as in Step 3. If old floors, sand parallel with boards. In general, work away from electric outlet, rather than toward it. Carry cable over shoulders to keep path clear.

6. Preparatory sanding with edger machine gets borders, closets, stairs ready for finish sanding. Use medium-grit sandpaper. This is first use of edger on new floors, or second use on old floors. Sanding operation is same for both, as in Step 4. After this step, all traces of old coatings should be gone. If not, use machines to clean up any low spots, finishing parallel with boards, before doing finish sanding.

7. Preparatory sanding with sanding block cleans up corners of borders, closets, stairs, and under radiators. Sand down and blend these spots with edges of adjoining areas. After this operation, completely clean up or vacuum sanding dust, and empty machine bags into covered containers.

8. Finish sanding with drum machine smooths broad areas for new coatings. Use fine-grit sandpaper. Before sanding, apply bleach to any spots as desired. Fill holes and cracks with plastic wood mixed to floor color with sanding dust. Wear soft footwear or remove shoes to avoid marks. Do complete sanding parallel with boards. This should smooth out all marks from previous sandings and give wood a velvet feel.

9. Finish sanding is completed with sanding block or shimmy pad sander, cleaning up corners of borders, closets, stairs, and under radiators. Then, completely clean up and vacuum sanding dust. Wear soft footwear or remove shoes. Prepare to apply first coating at once, or cover floor with clean papers to avoid marring. Thorough protection is important.

10. Coating with varnish brush and lamb's wool applicator. Apply coating according to maker's directions. Pour new finish into two large pans with clean paper under each. From one, start with brush, bordering about 6 inches wide so that applicator doesn't need to touch baseboard. From the other pan, follow with lamb's wool applicator, working parallel with boards, doing about 2-by-6-foot sections at a time.

11. Burnishing with a floor polisher between coats for a fine finish. First liquid coat on bare wood curls up numerous wood fibers. Later coats often show up dried bubbles and trapped particles, resulting in stiff, rough nibs. Thus the need for burnishing between coats. Use a floor pad, coarse, under polisher fitted with brush and holder. Burnish dry in sections of about 6 by 6 feet. Vacuum when done.

12. Polishing wax with floor polisher gives wood that new-floor beauty. Apply wax according to maker's directions. Use a fine floor pad with the machine. Buff and polish in sections of about 6 by 6 feet. Moisten the pad with water for highest luster. Thus you can choose the degree of polish desired.

All photos courtesy of the Norton Company.

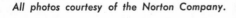

sanders—like most rotary mowers—have one side that cuts closer to obstructions than the other. Thus, you'll move tightly along a wall in one direction, and along the opposite wall in the other direction, parallel to the boards in both cases. At the ends, where the flooring butts into the walls, you must be careful not to let the big sander bump the baseboard while the drum is on the floor, or the sudden stop will produce a depression. Lift the drum just as the front of the sander reaches the baseboard.

With the floor sanded as close to the edges as possible with the bigger, faster, more efficient drum sander, switch to the disc sander. This machine usually rides on two casters, with the disc acting as the third support— although some models have no casters. The disc is housed, but an opening on the side away from the casters lets the sandpaper work up to a fraction of an inch away from the shoe mold. In some cases, you may want to take the shoe mold off, thus letting the disc sander work so close to the wall that the unsanded area will be covered when you put the molding back. However, this operation may make it necessary to refinish the baseboard, and if that is the case, there are easier methods (see below) of taking care of that narrow strip the sander won't reach.

In use, the casters on the sander are usually adjusted so that one edge of the disc is raised slightly, permitting you to steer the tool exactly where you want it. This is important, since the action of any disc sander is to produce swirl marks, and the less area you cover with such marks, the better.

Common practice is to work with the same grades of paper used on the big sander, although one grade finer at the finish of the edging work usually means a smoother job. This is particularly important if you are staining the floor, since the swirl marks take an abnormal amount of stain, making the edges look dark. If you have a belt sander or a jitter sander, use it along the edges wherever it will reach, to make the wood all the smoother.

At this point, you have a thin line of old finish right at the walls, and little places in all inside corners where the disc sander can't reach. The easiest way to clean up these areas is with a scraper, followed by sandpaper. As a last step, vacuum the floor thoroughly.

SELECTION OF FINISHES FOR FLOORS. The floor finishing materials you buy today from your paint dealer or from flooring specialty houses are infinitely superior to anything you could buy even a few years ago. They go on more easily, last longer, and are easier to maintain. What's more, they're more beautiful, and you are no longer saddled with the same old color. Woodhue stains are more and more popular, in a color more like walnut than anything else.

The most common types of finishes for floors are penetrating wood finishes, clear or colored; varnish, satin finish or glossy; shellac, and lacquer. Stains are feasible under the clear finishes, but are most workable under varnish. To discuss them one by one. . . .

Penetrating floor finishes. Every major paint manufacturer offers a penetrating finish that is either intended specifically for floors or formulated in such a way that it makes an excellent finish for all wood, including floors. These are handled by regular paint dealers. In addition there are specialists in floor finishes who make penetrating materials intended for use by commercial floor finishers. Quite often, the commercial finishers will sell you their materials—although you may find they'd prefer to merchandise it as part of their services.

The penetrating materials are by far the easiest to use of all floor finishes, requiring no skill, no equipment, no experience. To use them, you merely swab them on the floor, using a brush or a wad of cloth. Or— you pour them on the floor and spread them around with rags. The best way is to work in strips about as wide as you can reach. Swab on a strip. Keep an eye on it for half an hour, and as it soaks into the wood, add more finish, to keep it wet. Then wipe it all off. *All off.* Do another strip— and continue until the floor is done. The next day, repeat the process. (Some brands dry rapidly enough so you can do both coats in one day.)

The resulting finish is *in the wood,* not on the surface. The look is as though the wood were bare, although there is a slight darkening of natural woodhues and of course a change in color if you use a staining penetrating finish. What happens with these materials is a filling of wood pores with resins which harden, making the surface of the flooring extremely tough. Scratches never show unless they are very deep—deeper than the penetration of the finish. Water resistance is superb. Maintenance can be nil—or you can wash the floor if you want to. Penetrating finishes are slow to wear out, because you must actually wear away the wood to remove the finish. If, over a long period of time, it should wear through, you can spot-patch the worn areas with a repeat application of the same penetrating finish. The patch never shows.

Shellac. More shellac is sold for floors than for any other purpose. It has the advantage of flexibility, economy, and quick drying. When it is properly applied it wears well, except under hard-use situations. One of its best characteristics is "patchability." When a spot becomes worn, you can sand and clean it, then feather in a new shellac finish in a patch you can hardly see. (It is impossible to do this with varnish, although penetrating finishes are easy to patch.) The major disadvantage of shellac is a low resistance to water and other liquids. It must usually be carefully waxed—because much of its durability comes from the wax.

Most homeowners find shellac quite easy to work with and are pleased with its speed of drying. A 3-pound cut is recommended. Apply the first coat with full smooth flow, using a wide brush. Avoid puddling. Allow this coat to dry two hours. Apply filler if required, and allow plenty of drying time. Hand sand with 2/0 paper and dust. Recoat. Allow a second coat to dry three hours; if you put on a third coat, four hours before you walk on it. Sand with 2/0 before a third coat. Sand with 3/0 for a final smoothing. Wax twenty-four hours later. (Filler is rarely used with shellac, since the shellac fills the grain quite well in two- or three-coat jobs.)

A modified shellac floor finish which is not much harder to use than ordinary shellac but gives a much better performance is on the market under the trade name Target. It incorporates additional resins and makes use of a special hardener additive. Target is not offered by all paint dealers, but they should be able to order it for you from William Zinsser and Co., offices in New York and Chicago.

Varnish. Although the first coat of varnish may penetrate into the wood to a degree (particularly if it is properly thinned about 10 percent with turpentine or paint thinner), varnish is fundamentally an on-the-wood finish. When it wears or scratches off, it reveals bared wood. Patching is difficult. Abrasion resistance, however, is very high, particularly among the urethane formulas. Special high-build varnishes are made for floors, under the name of "gym" varnish, usually. These materials tend to yellow more quickly than the urethanes, which build less while providing superior wear resistance. Each coat of varnish takes at least twenty-four hours to dry.

The slow drying qualities of varnish, contributing to the way it is affected by inevitable dust in the air, make it one of the most difficult of all finishes to put on smoothly. In addition, the slow drying makes varnish a three- or four-day proposition. And the requirement that you must use a filler on oak for a true on-the-wood, smooth-and-level finish (see below). In total, it means you must truly desire a glassy finish on your floors if you will accept the work involved. Here is the schedule:

Thin the first coat of varnish with 1 part of thinner to 8 parts of varnish, except over a pigmented wiping stain. Apply successive coats at full strength. Flow the varnish on as smoothly as possible, laying on, brushing out, and tipping off each brushful. Avoid puddling. Look at the varnish from a low angle now and then, to make sure you are not skipping or puddling. Allow each coat of varnish twenty-four hours to dry. Sand with 2/0 sandpaper between coats. Dust carefully, and wipe with a turpentine-dampened rag between coats. Wax when wear starts to dull the surface—or immediately if you wish to delay wear.

Urethane varnishes: Use semigloss for final coat, to produce nongloss surface. Read labels for drying times, which are much faster with some urethanes than with regular varnishes.

Lacquer. One of the most widely used of all floor finishes is a special high-build material such as Fabulon, made by Pierce and Stevens in Buffalo, New York. It handles much the same as varnish, but drying time is much faster. You've got to be able to move along with it, and that is why floor lacquers are much more often used by professionals than by homeowners themselves. The volatiles are sometimes offensive and the product is extremely flammable. For that reason there is considerable fire hazard, and very good cross ventilation is essential. However, you can get two or more coats of lacquer on a floor in one day, and have the job finished, if you are aware of the dangers and take proper precautions.

Use no filler under lacquer, and no stain except spirit, water, or nongrain-raising varieties. Oil-based stains—as well as other oleo-resinous materials—are softened by the solvents in lacquer, and the result is short-lived. For the first coat, a special lacquer primer is suggested as optional for oak but required for pine and maple. Apply the first coat with a wide brush or a mohair roller. Work fast to prevent the double-build from area to area from producing lapmarks. Allow one hour for drying. Hand sand with 2/0, dust. Recoat. For two-coat work, allow overnight drying. For three coats, sand again with 2/0 and put on a third coat reduced with one part of thinner to four parts of lacquer. To avoid drying problems, use the thinner manufactured by the firm which made the lacquer. Allow overnight drying before traffic. Wax this finish when wear starts to make it dull.

When to use wood filler. The use of wood filler on floors is becoming less and less common, with the increasing appreciation of the natural look. Its purpose is to fill and level the open pores of such wood as oak, so the finish will be perfectly smooth, and the only time you should consider it is when you want glassy-glossy smooth floors. Many experts contend that fillers reduce the wear-resistance of subsequent finishes by providing a less than ideal substrate.

Never use fillers under shellac or lacquer. They defeat the purpose of penetrating finishes. What is left is varnish.

Filler goes on after the first, thinned coat of varnish. If the floor is stained, the filler must be tinted with the same color. If the natural shade of the wood is dark, it is most often best to tint the filler slightly, to avoid the look of wood pores lighter than the rest of the wood. In fact, many meticulous workers prefer to tint wood filler deliberately a tiny bit darker than the wood, to give the pores a subtle accenting.

Filler is paste-thick when you buy it, and should be thinned to a heavy brushing consistency with turpentine or paint thinner. Apply it with brush strokes first with the grain, then across it. Work in areas convenient to reach on your hands and knees. When the filler dulls over, indicating that the volatiles have evaporated and what remains is, again, paste-thick filler, wipe the material off with cross-grain strokes, using a heavy, open fabric such as burlap. *It is important to wipe clean,* since all you want is filler in the pores and *none on the surface.* When the filler is dry, rub your hand over the surface. If there is a toothy feel, your best bet is to go over the floor lightly with No. 3/0 (120-grit) sandpaper. Otherwise, your final finish will be, almost literally, glued to the floor with a weak film of filler.

Floor sanding sheets come in sizes to fit all popular floor machines.

FACTS ABOUT FLOOR FINISHES

Note: The following schedules are for bare floors—either new and sanded, or old with all finish removed and the dust vacuumed. If a stain is used, be sure it is compatible with topcoating. Full drying of finish is important. The time needed varies widely with temperature and humidity. Times given in chart below therefore are approximate.

Preparation	First Coat	Wood Filler	Second Coat	Third Coat	Wax
SHELLAC (3 LB. CUT)					
See note above. Use no oil stain	Brush on uniformly. Let dry 2 hr. Hand-sand with 2/0 paper. Dust	If desired	Let dry 3 hr. for recoat, 4 before walking on	Advisable over unfilled woods. Sand with 3/0	Apply as directed on container
LACQUER					
See note above. Use no oil stain. Apply special primer—optional for oak, required for pine and maple. Let dry well	Apply with brush or mohair roller. Work fast to avoid lap marks. Dry 1 hr. Hand-sand with 2/0. Dust	No filler required unless pores are very large	Let dry overnight if final coat. For 3rd coat, sand after 3 hr. and dust	Reduce: 3 parts lacquer to 1 part thinner	Not essential until wear begins to roughen surface
PENETRATING WOOD FINISH**					
See note above	Brush, roll, or swab it on. Let penetrate 20 to 30 min. Wipe off excess. Let dry, following directions on label	If desired. Usually not used	Same as first coat. Let dry according to label directions	Not needed	If desired
VARNISH					
See note above	Thin 1 part thinner to 8 parts varnish. Brush or roll on. Let dry with 2/0. Dust	Use if smoothest surface is desired	Apply full strength. Let dry 24 hr. For 3rd coat hand-sand and dust	Apply full strength if desired. Let dry 24 hr.	Immediately—or delay until wear begins to dull surface
POLYURETHANE VARNISH*					
See note above	Apply with brush or roller. Let dry 6-8 hr. Sand with 3/0. Use clear to build finish	Use no filler	Use clear for glossy look or to build finish. Dry and sand as before	If satin finish is desired, use it for final coat only	Optional
VINYL VARNISH					
See note above. Seal wood with 3-lb. shellac. Dry 2 hr., sand, dust	Brush on in a smooth even coating	If desired	Apply after 2 hr. and before 6. If latter is impossible, wait 48 hr.	Not needed	Optional

TWO COMPONENT VARNISH

See note above. Use no oil stain	Brush on full strength (for maple, reduce 1 to 4). Let dry 3 hr. Hand-sand with 2/0. Dust	See maker's instructions	Brush on. Let dry 4-6 hr. Sand and dust before 3rd coat	Required for pine. Let final coat dry 48 hr. before waxing. (Cure takes two weeks)	As direct-ed on con-tainer

*One-coat method: Swab material on rapidly; keep surface wet for 30 to 60 minutes by adding more material as dry spots appear. Then wipe clean and dry. **Commercial method:** Contractors buff penetrating sealer into the wood with #2 steel wool on a machine, instead of wiping. **Important:** Spread wiping rags to dry outdoors. They're a fire hazard.

**Be sure to read labels of all "plastic" varnishes carefully. Some recommended special fillers. Some have instructions not common to all brands.

STAINING THE WOOD FLOOR. Owing to the trends toward floors that are a medium-dark brown in color, you may want to stain yours. If you do, the process comes immediately after sanding, before any other finishing material goes on. Here are the common methods and materials for staining wood floors:

Pigmented wiping stains. The prototype material is Minwax, which most paint outlets sell, although equivalent materials are produced by just about every paint manufacturer. These stains are, typically, an oleoresinous vehicle with a relatively small resin content, in which there are colorants both in solution and in suspension. Thus, they must be stirred well, before and during use. The pigmented wiping stains are perfectly easy to use. You just brush them on, wait a while, then wipe off. The depth of staining depends on how long you leave them on before wiping off. However, if the color is a little too dark, it is better to thin the stain with turpentine and give it adequate penetration time than to wipe it too soon. Conversely, if you want a darker color than the stain gives you with normal procedures, do not leave it too long before wiping, or you may end up with a mottled, unpleasant look. Instead, apply a second coat after the first is dry.

It is important to wipe the surface of the flooring clean, so that the wood grain shows clearly. Otherwise, you are effectively "painting" the wood with a thin, opaque coating.

To make sure subsequent topcoatings do not soften the stain, let it dry thoroughly. Overnight is usually okay. *Remember:* it is not wise to put lacquer or shellac over pigmented wiping stains. On the other hand, their moderate resin content makes them function somewhat as a sealer for varnish and as a semi-first-application of penetrating wood finish. You may find that you need one fewer topcoats.

Colored penetrating sealers. Some of the commercial penetrating finishes come in woodhues, as mentioned earlier. You can, also, add colors in oil or universal pigments to clear penetrating finishes. This is, generally, more difficult and no more satisfactory than using pigmented wiping stains, unless you cannot find the color you want in any ready-mixed brand. Count on a considerable investment in pigment, if you set out to make a staining material out of a clear pigmented finish; it takes a lot.

Interesting floor colors which are not woodhues are in frequent use these days. Green, blue, and other colors can be applied in the form of stains which you mix yourself with pigments and penetrating finishes.

Stains. You can use regular nongrain-raising or water stains. These will give you the best, clearest, and most permanent colors. They are the best under lacquer topcoatings, and produce superb colors under penetrating finishes, shellacs, or varnishes of any kind.

Colored varnish. If the color you like best happens to come from a colored varnish, experiment on a sample of wood until you find how much dilution the color will stand, using turpentine or paint thinner. Thinned, the varnish will penetrate and carry much of its color into the wood. Then, topcoat with a good varnish system. Don't use lacquer over the colored varnish.

WHICH FINISH IS BEST FOR YOU? A summarization of the qualities of various finishes may help you decide which suits your needs. When you select a finish for a floor, you must do it on the basis of the most important considerations:

From the standpoint of *wear,* the best on-the-surface material is a moisture-cure urethane. This stuff is so tough they use it on warehouse floors, where it takes the beating of wheeled moving equipment. It has a surface about as glossy as varnish, a good color, only slight yellowing. It has a disadvantage, however. To make the material brushable, they usually use xylene. The vapors are toxic. Without plenty of moving air, they could produce unconsciousness. Never use it without ventilation—and that means more than just cracking a window an inch or two. Open two doors to be safe.

Oil-modified urethane or "polyurethanes" are only slightly less wear-resistant than their moisture-curing cousins. They come as satin or semigloss, and for that reason are a prime choice for fashionable floors.

The best finish *in the wood* from the wear standpoint is the special floor sealer mentioned above. When you use one of these finishes properly, there is just about no reason why the floors shouldn't look good for the life of the house, with ordinary care.

Best from the *beauty* standpoint depends quite a bit on the eye of the beholder. The plain, untouched look of in-the-wood finishes is considered loveliest by most people, followed by the satin look of the nongloss varnish, getting advantages of both. The in-the-wood finish proves an excellent base for the satin-finish urethane. Much of the patchability of the in-the-wood is gained by this method, too, since the wood *under* the varnish carries the varnish color deeper than just the surface.

Best as to *ease of application* is, again, the penetrating finish. You merely brush it on, let it sink in a while, then wipe it off. Second easiest is shellac, applied as several coats. Lacquer is harder than shellac, but less difficult than varnish. Most difficult of all are the moisture-curing or catalytic varnishes. The actual difficulty of use is no greater with these materials than with ordinary varnish; the problems they offer are the need for ventilation with its attendant perils, and the chance that the materials may harden before a moderately slow worker can handle them.

Best as to *maintenance* can be decided only by dividing maintenance into two phases:

1. What is easiest to keep looking decent with the least time and trouble?

2. What is easiest to repair, if there is serious damage not involving the entire floor?

A good glossy varnish is very easy to keep clean and gleaming if it is not scratched, and particularly if it is not scratched through to the wood. Most dirt just wipes up. This is also true of lacquer. Semigloss materials don't show scratches as much as glossies, of course. Minor scratching can be kept invisible with wax—if the scratches are not too deep. Also, wax on a new varnish floor provides a sort of lubrication which forestalls scratching. In-the-wood finishes don't show scratches less serious than those you might suffer through some such action as someone dragging a nail across the floor.

Shellac and penetrating finishes are leaders in touchup. You can wear out the spots in front of a door, the edges of stair treads, and other heavy wear areas, then touch them up easily with either of these materials. It is much more difficult to do this with varnish, lacquer, and other on-the-surface finishes. Lacquer floor finishes can be touched up all right provided the problem is wear—not failure of adhesion.

CHAPTER EIGHT

HOW TO MAKE THE MOST OF COLOR

COLOR FOR THE INTERIOR. You like some colors better than others. You have formulated—consciously or unconsciously—ideas about what colors are appropriate for certain uses and inappropriate for others. This makes you a color expert, insofar as your home and its furnishings are concerned. To use the shades and hues you like best to their best advantage, it helps if you make use of scientific and psychological facts about color, developed through research. With these facts you can:

- Use color to make a room seem warmer or cooler to be in.
- Change the apparent size or shape of a room by the use of colors and patterns.
- Draw attention to extra good features about your house and home— to draw attention away from bad features.
- Establish the mood of a room, making it quiet and dignified, happy and gay—young in spirit or more mature.

Colors are cool or warm. You need only think of a few common expressions in our language to realize how much the warm or cold nature of various colors influences us. We use "red hot," "ice blue," "cool green," "flame yellow," and others because the temperature and the color go together. As you know, one half the color spectrum is called "cold" and the other "warm."

This explains one of the basic rules of color selection in the home:

Use warm colors in rooms with northern and eastern exposure; use cool colors in rooms with southern and western exposure.

You know how this works if you'll imagine yourself sitting in a room on a hot summer day, with the sunlight pouring in—and the walls painted a rose color. Reverse the situation to a room with a northern exposure, on a cold winter day, and the walls done in pale blue-green.

Keep this factor in mind as you select colors. Choose among your favorites in hues of green, blue, violet, yellow-green, blue-green, and blue-violet for rooms in which abundant sunlight will contribute a natural warmth. For rooms where sunlight will be scarce, hues of red, yellow,

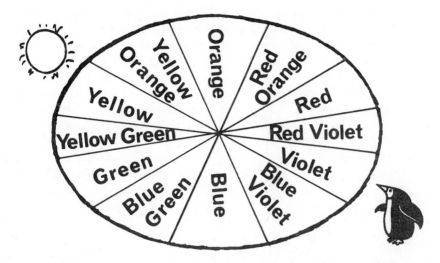

Color gives the effect of warmth or coolness to the person who looks at it. Warm colors are usually recommended for north exposures, somewhat dark rooms. Cool colors should be your choice if a room has plenty of bright sunlight.

orange, yellow-orange, red-orange, and red-violet help make up for the lack of warmth in the lighting.

Colors affect apparent size. One common optical-illusion trick is to display two balls of identical size, one red and one green or blue. "Which ball is bigger?" is the question. Red always wins, because objects colored red (and to a lesser degree the other colors on the warm side of the color wheel) seem *bigger* and *closer* than things colored from the other side of the wheel.

You can take advantage of this phenomenon if you remember that a warm-colored room seems smaller—the walls seem closer—than a cool-colored room. Whenever such circumstances as orientation need not be the controlling factor, you can give a small room a little seeming size by using colors from the cool side of the color wheel.

The depth of the color is a factor here, too. Light colors make a room seem bigger, while darker shades seem to bring the walls in closer. Thus, a pale pink room might seem larger than a darker green room, despite the coolness of the green. Thus, the depth of color makes a great deal of difference, when you are seeking to make a room seem bigger. White, for example, makes a room seem biggest of all.

Even when your rooms are of a size that make the effects of color no factor, you can often use light and cool colors to make a hallway or stairs seem wider.

Pattern is a factor in making rooms seem larger or smaller, too. When you are leafing through the book of wallpaper patterns, keep in mind that a large, pronounced, or busy design will have the effect of seeming closer to you than milder paper.

Even when your rooms are big enough so that the effects of color and pattern are not critical, you can often take advantage of light and cool shades to make a hallway or a stairway seem wide—and you can avoid using a heavy pattern in wallpaper which might make a hallway seem narrow.

Colors affect the apparent shape of a room. When you want to change the shape or proportions of a room through the use of color, take advantage of the way warm or dark colors (or conspicuous patterns, in the case of wallpaper) seem to be closer to you. A long, narrow room can be made to seem shorter if the end walls are treated in a way that brings them in. For example, a room painted in a light, cool shade might have end walls papered. The effect does not have to be striking for this trick to work. It can be done with white paint on two of the walls, and a very subtle pattern or a soft warm shade on the end walls. It is not usually necessary or desirable to treat both end walls of this sort of room. Most often, one of the walls is likely to have windows or a door, which give it some life; and, most often, you spend the majority of the time toward one end, making the other end the one which should be treated to shorten the room.

This effect works the other way, too. It is possible to give a room the feeling of greater width if a side wall is treated with cool, light, or white colors.

Color can emphasize good features. One of the best tricks in the interior decorator's bag is to create a background of color for a particularly attractive piece of furniture or a grouping. An example of this would be to dramatize, let's say, a breakfront or a modern teak shelf-and-storage unit. If you were to place the furniture between two windows with draperies ceiling to floor, and give the wall back of the furniture a carefully selected complementary color, you'd set if off in a way that showed it better than it really is.

This is done, too, with wallpaper. A room might have plain painted walls, but back of a special grouping, a stunning wallpaper provides extra drama. In fact, when budget is a consideration, it is feasible to use a small area in a wall covering you couldn't afford for the whole room. Sometimes this wallpaper background is done in the form of an isolated panel, surrounded with molding to separate it from the rest of the wall.

Color establishes the mood of a room. The colors on the warm side of the color wheel are the lively, happy, active colors. On the cool side, the colors are calm, sedate, dignified. These characteristics help suggest the best colors for certain rooms—and for certain people, because they affect people, both emotionally and physically. Here are the effects of several colors, based on research by leading paint and wallpaper manufacturers:

• Red is exciting, warm, virile. It suggests and promotes movement and increased muscular activity. The medical profession has found that red stimulates breathing and blood pressure. Red is a young color. Too much of it is overpowering, and it is usually reserved for accents. Its brightness and attention-getting qualities are the reasons for its wide use in children's surroundings; it generally draws reactions from infants sooner than other colors.

- Orange is like red—only a little less so. It, too, must be used in relatively small doses, although fairly large splotches of orange are sometimes attractive accents. In modern decorating, orange is often used for what you might call its shock value—many times all the more shocking in combinations with blues and purples.

- Yellow is the cheerful color, particularly useful in northern exposure situations. Its light reflectance is excellent, making it great for rooms with too few windows, students' rooms where good illumination is important, and similar cases. Yellow in its more intense shades can have the same overpowering effect as red. Soft yellows, however, are quite restful.

- Green and shades of green are the tranquilizing colors. They produce a restful effect, and range from a fair degree of warmth toward the very yellowish greens to considerable coolness among the bluish greens. Green is the most comfortable color on earth—for the reason that it is the most common color on earth. Since it is so common, and so neutral, it tends to become monotonous and product boredom if it is overused, particularly in some of the wishy-washy lighter shades.

- Medical findings indicate that, just the opposite of red, blue tends to decrease muscular tension and reduce blood pressure and to slow down breathing and pulse rates.

- Purple gets the nod from very few color authorities, who point out that it is pompous, aloof, austere.

- Gray, the neutral color, is neutral in its effect on people. It is excellent background for colorful decorations, to which it gives emphasis through its own lack of prominence. When grays are too dark, however, they are sombre and depressing and demand a great deal of color accent to enliven them.

What colors for what rooms? Color authorities believe that certain colors are more appropriate for one room of the house than another:

- Living rooms can be done in warm colors, which make them gay and dynamic . . . or in cool colors which make them more restful.

- Bedrooms, more than any other areas of a home, are personal rooms and should be done in the favorite colors of the occupant. Young people often prefer warm colors in bedrooms, while adults lean toward neutral and cool colors. It is not considered good practice to work too much excitement in color or pattern into sleeping rooms.

- Dining rooms call for light browns, greens toward the yellow side, peach tones, and deep rose or raspberry reds. These colors are known to stimulate the appetite and make food look attractive. Yellows are good in dining rooms, the popularity of candlelight illumination being one of the reasons why.

- Kitchens should be as cheerful as possible—but never overlook the inevitable heat from cooking. Compound this with a "hot" color scheme

Complimentary colors always go well together without offending any eye. They are any colors opposite each other on the color wheel.

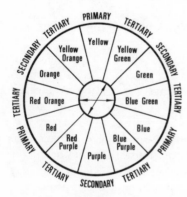

Split complementaries take advantage of the closeness of two colors flanking one of the opposites, as this drawing shows. You could turn the Y 180 degrees for the opposite split complementaries.

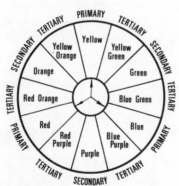

Double complementaries use the hues flanking both of the opposites. This gives you the extreme versatility of a four-color scheme.

The triad system of color scheming is widely used. Any three colors on the wheel determined in this manner are sure to work well together.

and the kitchen can become physically and mentally unbearable. Color experts suggest pale buffs, yellows, greens, blues, beige.

Although it is hazardous to attempt to establish trends in a book such as this, which will be read over a period of many years, it is safe to say that the most popular color for walls in every room is white, or very light off-white. This has been true since the beginning of the 1960s and a little before. The popularity of white will no doubt continue, for it provides the perfect background for all kinds of colors of furniture, pictures, draperies, and other items of decoration.

White does not necessarily mean pure, simple white. In fact, most white wall paints contain traces of pigments, so that they are actually colors. Thus, a white may be warm or cool, depending on whether it is taken "off-white" with warm or cool pigments. In many paint lines, however, there is a special paint called "ceiling white" with little or no off-white pigmentation. It is usually quite flat, and the white, nonsheen surface tends to remove the ceiling entirely from the visual context. You never notice it, you never know it's there.

COLOR ON THE OUTSIDE OF YOUR HOUSE. If it is true that more interiors are white than any other color, it is doubly true that more exteriors are white than any other color. You can drive down the streets of town after town and see nothing but white houses. There has been a slight trend toward colors in recent years—a trend that is quite regional, rarely the same in two parts of the country. For instance, the West and Southwest show a considerable use of pastel colors. The East and the Northeast have gone toward darker colors, including the dark reds, ochres, and greens of Colonial times.

When you choose a color for your house, there are a few main considerations.

It is always easiest to maintain the existing color, or one not much lighter or darker. This is true not only because you can easily "carry" the old color in one coat, but also because the new paint (let's say white over white) seems to last longer. This is due to the fact that when it weathers and gets thin, what shows through is the same color—and you can't see it. If the color change is great (say charcoal over white) you may be able to get away with one coat, but probably not unless you are a very skillful painter. Moreover, when the new paint weathers only a little bit, the contrasting white substrate starts to show through.

It is best to consider your neighbors and neighborhood when you choose a paint. This is not to suggest that individuality is to be submerged in favor of conformity. But, you do your neighbors no favor to put them on either side of a house that looks out of place—and you do yourself no favor either.

Natural surroundings are a factor, too. If your house sits in a grove of trees, or on a rocky rise, or a flat urban lot, or in a big open development, the color considerations are different. The green background would accept

Here are some suggested color schemes for your home:

If your house has shutters, paint the trim the same color as body of house—or white. If not, use these suggested colors for trim.

If the roof of your house is	You can paint the body	...and the trim or shutters and doors															
		Pink	Bright red	Red-orange	Tile red	Cream	Bright yellow	Light green	Dark green	Gray-green	Blue-green	Light blue	Dark blue	Blue-gray	Violet	Brown	White
GRAY	White	X	X	X	X	X	X	X	X	X	X	X	X	X	X	X	
	Gray	X	X	X	X			X	X	X	X	X	X	X	X	X	X
	Cream-yellow		X		X		X		X	X							X
	Pale green				X		X		X	X							X
	Dark green	X				X	X	X									X
	Putty			X	X				X	X		X	X		X		
	Dull red	X			X		X						X				X
GREEN	White	X	X	X	X	X	X	X	X	X	X	X	X	X	X	X	X
	Gray		X		X	X	X										X
	Cream-yellow		X		X			X	X	X						X	X
	Pale green		X	X		X		X		X							X
	Dark green	X	X			X	X	X									X
	Beige			X					X	X	X		X	X			
	Brown	X				X	X	X									X
	Dull red					X		X		X							X
RED	White		X		X				X		X		X				
	Light gray		X		X				X								X
	Cream-yellow		X		X						X	X	X				
	Pale green		X		X												X
	Dull red					X		X		X	X						X
BROWN	White		X	X			X	X	X	X	X		X	X	X		
	Buff			X					X	X	X					X	
	Pink-beige			X					X	X						X	X
	Cream-yellow			X					X	X	X					X	
	Pale green			X					X	X						X	
	Brown		X		X	X											X
BLUE	White		X	X		X						X	X				
	Gray		X	X								X	X				X
	Cream-yellow		X	X								X	X				
	Blue		X			X	X						X				X

almost any color, but the best choice would be one with about the same value as the trees—value being the colorist's word for "depth" or "darkness." A gray house on the rocky rise would blend well into its background, and bright accents in shutters, outdoor furniture, window boxes or other accessories would be set off dramatically. Pastels in unobstrusive shades would be a good choice for the urban lot. In the big development, if it follows much of the recent trend, the sky may be the limit. Many developers in recent years have hired color specialists to pick the colors to be used on every house in the neighborhood. Quite often there has been color galore. Usually, however, all the colors are compatible as to value, hue, and chroma. Any house that departed from the theme would be conspicuous, indeed.

In the past, the color of a roof has always been a determining factor. A house might have asphalt shingles in green, red, white, or some other color, restricting the selection of color for the house, itself. Nowadays, however, this has been changed by the fact that you can paint the asphalt roof, using latex paints.

Color can change the shape of a house. Just as color can be used to alter the apparent shape of a room inside, color can change the shape and apparent size of an entire house. For example, a dark-colored house always seems smaller than one that is light. Houses painted with shades on the cool side of the color wheel seem smaller. Warm hues make them seem bigger. You'll recognize these factors as being the same that alter sizes and shapes indoors.

It goes even farther than that. You can make a house seem lower if you avoid emphasizing vertical lines, and in fact, put emphasis on horizontal lines. For example, corner boards painted in contrasting trim color seem higher than boards the same as the body of the house. If your house happens to be one of the common "broken roofline" styles—that is, with one section two stories, another one story—you can work considerable miracles in its shape.

To make the two-story section higher, paint it all one color, with the wing different.

To make the two-story section lower, paint the house all one color, or paint the lower half one color and the second-story section another.

Sometimes a house has unattractive features—structural elements that may have seemed good when the house was built, but now are outdated. You can make such features less conspicuous by painting them the same color as the rest of the house, regardless of trim. For instance, if there is an overpowering porch, don't follow the natural-seeming course of painting its columns and trim an accent color although there may be contrasting trim elsewhere. Conversely, when there are exceedingly good architectural features, you can emphasize them by deliberately changing their color. This is part of the theory back of entranceways painted a color unlike that of the rest of the house.

Perhaps the most common need for "burying" a feature occurs on houses with a huge chimney at one end. As a pile of bricks, it may be an eyesore. With modern latex paints, you can paint masonry as readily as wood—so you merely "paint the chimney in," and being the same color as its background, it disappears. This technique works, too, with the entirely opposite problem: the single-flue chimney up the end of a house, too small to be a feature, worthy only of being covered up.

Another feature is odd window size. Frequently the windows on at least one side of the house had to be positioned with the emphasis on function, without regard to size, shape, balance. When you have this problem, do not paint the trim in a different color on these offbeat windows, even though you use a trim paint elsewhere.

No discussion of color should ever come to an end without emphasis on the fact that there is only one real color expert in the world: you. You know what you like, what pleases you. If it pleases you, use it. However, don't let your "color education" stand complete as it is. Be a constant student of color and its effects, so you can always utilize color to the fullest extent of its value both decoratively and emotionally.

CHAPTER NINE

WHEN TO PAINT YOUR HOUSE

YOU GET a great deal of personal satisfaction out of painting your own house. It's a job that *shows*. And it contributes value both in the way it makes the place look better and in the way it protects the materials the house is made of.

But—painting just for the fun of it is no fun, and it does not contribute in either the beautifying or the protective sense. If you paint oftener than you should, you do more harm than good. In fact, experts can prove that it is worse to paint too often than too infrequently.

There is a right time to paint your house. You may never be able to pinpoint this time precisely, but there are methods of coming close. Think about it is this way: If you wait too long before you paint, the old paint may be in very bad shape. It may have deteriorated so badly that extensive pre-painting work is necessary. It may have weathered to such an extent that you need two coats—or more—to rebuild a sound coating.

On the other hand, if you repaint too often you are sure to build up a coating that is too thick, brittle, prone to chip and crack. As the structure of the house comes and goes with variation in humidity and temperature, this over-thick coating can't keep up with the change. It forms cracks and "alligatoring" clear through to the wood, exposing it to weathering and decay.

Here are the facts about paint-film thickness and frequency of painting:

When a house is first built and first painted, it usually has three coats. The first is the primer. Then, there is a two-coat topcoating. With the high-quality paints on the market today, this usually means a "build" of about 7 mils—7/1000 of an inch. A film this thick is normally capable of moving with the wood beneath it; 7 mils is considered about ideal.

Careful tests by paint chemists reveal that the coating on the house weathers away at the rate of about a half mil every year or a little faster. This means that at the end of a five-year period, the coating is down to about 4 or 5 mils. At this point, you can put it back up to about 7 mils with a good one-coat house paint. Two coats might be too much. This complement of weathering and recoat thickness is the basis for the properly popular one-coat painting schedule. (The actual time required for a weather-off of 3 mils depends on many factors, as will be seen; vital among them is the slower weathering rate of some of our top-grade latex house paints.)

HOW PAINT GOES BAD. It is easiest to analyze the need for repaint if you understand and take into consideration the stages a new paint job goes through on the road to ruin. This process is typical of oil-paint finishes and occurs with slight variations and a greater time lag with latex paints.

The first stage is soiling. When an oil paint dries, it has an oil-glossy surface which, though dry, is slightly tacky. Dirt, dust, smoke and other soil which come into contact with this sticky surface adhere. In a few weeks a newly painted house may have a disappointingly dirty look about it. Fortunately, as the paint cures, this adhesive surface disappears—washes away—and the dirt with it. The house starts to look decent again.

This washing off of the glossy surface is called "flatting," and it is the beginning of the "chalking" period. Modern oil paints do not chalk as much as former formulas, and most latex paints do not chalk at all, in the accepted sense. However, today's oil paints chalk rapidly enough to keep themselves clean. What is chalking? The binders in the paint slowly decompose upon exposure to the weather. This releases the pigments, which are actually very fine powder, and they wash off with ordinary rainfall. Any dirt which may have lodged on the surface washes off, too. This action is

This is an excellent example of paint that has weathered too long before repainting. The dark color was applied over a white primer — and the primer shows through. The wood now needs two coats; you could not get by on a one-coat repaint schedule.

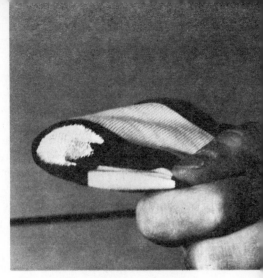

Excessive chalking is easy to detect by the "T-shirt method." Double the knit material over your finger and rub it for about 8 inches. If the chalk fills the fabric, you have an excessive amount of chalk. The house should be hosed down with a detergent. *Photo courtesy DuPont.*

the basis for the term "self-cleaning paint" which some manufacturers use to describe their products.

Controlled chalking continues over a period of three or four or more years. It is this gradual sluicing away of the paint which reduces the original 7-mil coating to the 4-mil level, ready for repaint. The process is formulated into the paint purposely, to eliminate as far as possible the chance that too thick a coating will build up with recoating.

Despite these precautions—and particularly with some cheap paints or some old-fashioned formulas—too much build is possible in certain locations. As a quick example, under a wide overhang there might not be enough rain to wash off the loosened chalk.

In such situations—or when you paint too often—the build is relatively great and as the paint ages it grows brittle. (This is less true of the more elastic latex formulas. With changes in humidity and temperature the wood expands and contracts, the brittle paint cracks and quickly deteriorates as moisture gets behind it to the wood. It chips, peels, flakes. The thicker the paint is the more likely this is to happen.

TWO WAYS TO LOOK AT THE OLD PAINT. Not all of the stages of deterioration happen at the same time. They may vary from one house to another. Almost surely they will vary from one side of a house to another. There are variations between different parts of the country. And—the job one painter does may not go bad as fast as that of another painter.

These inconsistencies make it necessary to examine your house in two ways, looking for painting need. First, you must keep the place under general observation all the time, checking the overall condition of the paint. Second, you must make closer inspections from time to time, in search of areas which are not keeping step with the rest of the house. You may find places where the paint is failing at an alarming rate; they obviously cannot wait for the rest of the house before they are taken care of. You may find other areas where there seems to be absolutely no deterioration of the paint. This in itself is a problem as vital—although not as difficult—as early failure. What must be done about these situations is covered in a later chapter. Obviously, early deterioration must be taken care of before you paint the whole house. Ordinarily, when you correct them they don't recur.

Meanwhile, there are certain clues you can spot easily which tell you when the overall job must be done. They are true indications that the topcoating (the two coats of paint over the primer) is wearing away, that it is getting so thin it no longer protects—or beautifies. As you look for these clues, keep in mind that paint should *never* be allowed to weather away to the point where the primer is exposed and, itself, begins to weather. If you wait that long before you paint, you may be letting yourself in for a three-coat renovation.

Grain show-through. As the paint weathers, the texture of the wood tends to show. It is probable that it has always been visible under the paint, particularly if the siding is southern pine, fir, or flat-sawn cedar. However, as the paint film gets thinner, the texture becomes more pronounced—sharper.

Brushmarks. Even though you are a good painter and put the coating on smoothly, there is a tendency for the pigment in the paint to align with the brush strokes. As the paint wears, this lineup of the pigment becomes visible, particularly under very strong cross lighting.

Primer show-through. It is by all means time to paint—probably with two coats—when you can start to detect the primer through the topcoat. There is always a difference in color between primer and topcoat, even when they are ostensibly the same—such as white. The reason for this is a difference in the pigments used in primers. Some painters even deliberately tint a primer very slightly off color, to make topcoating easier. This, of course, makes primer show-through detection easier.

Color fading. You may not be able to utilize this clue if your house is a light color. Dark paints, however, owe much of their color density to the thickness of the film, and they lighten considerably as the film thins. In some cases, particularly if a custom-color paint is not properly and thoroughly mixed, you may be able to detect a definite color change. As the paint dries, there may be a degree of stratification of the pigments. Naturally, as the paint weathers, different strata are exposed.

Dingy, dirty look. Most of the time, when a house looks dirty, it may not be any indication at all that it needs painting. Chances are that what you diagnose as dirt is, actually, mildew. It comes off with a bath of Clorox in water. When the dirty look has gone, there may be other indications that it's time to paint. Mildew is a major nuisance in keeping a house looking decent. If you are bothered with it, be sure to use a mildew-resistant material when you repaint.

Most of the foregoing applies to fairly recent paints, manufactured with a repaint schedule in mind. It does not apply so patly to very old houses. If your house is old, it may have a heavy build-up of paint, owing to the use in years past of obsolete paint types which did not offer controlled weathering. When this is the case you will often find severe cross-

Very often a house that looks like it needs painting is only dirty. Sponging and hosing remove normal dirt quickly. If detergents won't remove the dirt, chances are it is mildew, which can be removed with Clorox. *Photo courtesy DuPont.*

grain cracking of the paint. If the place has been carelessly maintained, someone may have painted over the cross-grain cracks—heedless of the fact that they will inevitably open again. Many times the only long-lived answer to the old, much painted house is to remove all the paint and start over with a modern three-coat system.

If your house is not much over twenty or twenty-five years old take the advice of the experts who say:

The best time to paint a house is just before it needs it.

Follow this recommendation and you will neither build up an over-thick coating, nor will you ever let the paint go so far that it's a back-breaking job to restore it.

CHAPTER TEN

GETTING YOUR HOUSE READY TO PAINT

MANY BRUSH strokes from now, you'll be finished. A big job. When you paint your house, you want to be sure you do it right. The proper preparations and application now can mean you won't have to open a paint can again for six, seven, eight years, except for possible touchup.

Doing it right means, more than anything else, getting the place ready to paint. Paint experts agree that most paint failure is caused by putting a topcoat over an improper substrate (a word meaning, among paint experts, "what you paint over"). Furthermore the paint failure is likely to repeat and repeat, unless you not only repair the superficial damage but also remedy the basic reason for failure.

THE PERIODIC CHECKUP. Every homeowner should form the habit of looking critically at his house several times a year. These checkups can be formal inspections—like periodic trips to see the doctor—or simply a matter of paying attention as you engage in normal activities around the house and yard.

On these inspections, you must keep an eye on the general condition of the house, looking for signs that the last paint job is eroding away—as was discussed in the previous chapter. In addition, you must watch carefully for signs of *early deterioration*—localized failure demanding more or less immediate action whether the whole house happens to need painting or not. Such deterioration usually takes one of these forms:

• Blistering, caused by the pressure of water in the wood trying to escape.

• Peeling, most often caused by the application of a new material over an unsuited substrate. The adhesion is bad. Beneath the peeling paint, the primer or other substrate is still adhering. "Tissue paper peeling" shows up where paint has been protected from normal weathering; it's actually peeled paint, tissue paper thin.

• Scaling, caused again by water for the most part. Sometimes it is the result of long-neglected blistering. More often it is caused by water entering the wood through cracks or openings in the "skin" of the house. Sometimes its cause goes clear back to the original painting, if it was done when there was moisture in the wood.

Form the habit of scrutinizing your house now and then, looking for general deterioration of the finish — and more particularly for localized failure that may need immediate attention. *Photo courtesy DuPont.*

- Alligatoring is paint cracked or crazed in two directions, and it usually happens when a film builds too thick and cannot accommodate the swelling and shrinking of the wood beneath it.
- Cross-grain cracking—long, single cracks, usually fairly evenly spaced, crosswise of the siding—is also due to overthick paint layer which becomes hard and brittle. This defect, as well as alligatoring, is most often found on fairly old houses, painted many times, with old-fashioned paints.
- Splintering, actual deterioration of siding and sometimes shingles, is a fault of the way the wood was handled at the sawmill. The best siding shows the edge grain on the surface. When the flat grain forms the surface, it is subject to swelling and shrinking—and splintering. This is particularly true when the flat grain which is outermost happens to be the side which was innermost in the growing tree. (Wood technologists call this the "bark side" vs. the "pith side.")
- Knots or pitch streaks improperly handled when the wood was first painted may continue to bleed their resin through painting after painting, may prevent some paints from drying at all, and eventually deteriorate, leaving cracks in the surface. (The standard method of getting rid of the knot and pitch problems is to coat them with shellac, which seals the resins.)
- Actual decay of the wood beneath the finish, almost always due to aggravated moisture conditions, quite often in secluded corners where air movement is slight, and near the bottom of exterior walls back of shrubbery. It is quite common whenever wooden siding or shingles come to within 6 or 8 inches of the ground.

Although these defects vary in their apparent seriousness, they have one thing in common: you cannot paint over them and forget them. If you do, they'll continue and they'll grow.

Let's start with the worst first. If your house is old and shows a great deal of alligatoring and cross-grain cracking, the amount of work involved is almost more than a homeowner can handle, himself. The job should go to a professional. But—before you decide to have a commercial painting outfit come in and strip the siding down to bare wood (that's what has to be done), get prices, too, from a contractor for aluminum siding, shingles, or some other method of dodging the issue entirely. Quite often,

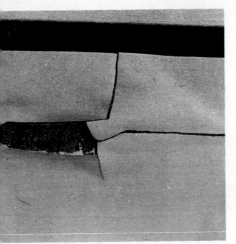

When paint peels to the bare wood, it is the primer which failed because it didn't do its job of adhesion and forming a perfect substrate for topcoats. Primers fail because they may not be properly selected, but more often because they are applied over wood which contains moisture. Solution: scrape to bare wood.

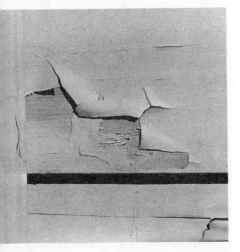

When paint peels down to the primer, it is a signal that the primer is okay, generally, but the topcoat did not adhere to it. This may be due to incompatibility between primer and topcoat. It may also be due to dirt on the primer, if it stood too long before topcoating. Solution: Scrape loose paint down to tightly adhering primer.

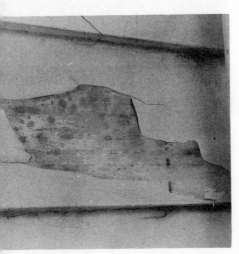

When paint peels down to a dirty gray surface, it is a sign that mildew has set in on the substrate and no paint will stick to it. Solution: scrape all loose paint, kill the mildew with a Clorox solution, use a mildew-resistant paint or additive. If you live in a warm, damp area, take special pains to combat mildew.

the cost of a new outside facing material is close to—sometimes less than—that of a difficult repaint job on a house in bad condition. An advantage in the new material is your choice among several varieties, many of them prefinished with factory-applied materials that carry a guarantee for many more years than you could expect from paint.

If your decision is to go for repainting, remember that the old paint must come off. The situation, caused by overbuilding of film in the first place, cannot be licked by building it even thicker. The best way to get old paint off is to shop around for a paint scraper with a built-in electrical unit. Some paint and hardware stores handle them, or could order one for you. In use, this instrument is moved slowly across the surface, so that the heating element softens the paint, then the scraper blade takes it off. Another version by Red Devil has only the heater; use any scraper. Following such scraping, you clean up with a smaller scraper, then sandpaper. Your object is clean, bare wood. You want a fresh start.

Do not use a blowtorch to remove paint from your house without seriously considering the fire hazard. Many, many homes have burned because a blowtorch used for paint removal shot its flame through cracks, into the interior of walls, setting fires that could not be put out before they had done tremendous damage. You are unwise even to let a commercial outfit use torches.

If the area which needs to be stripped is not too large, you can take paint off with a disc sander, although you end up with quite a bit of scraping where the sander can't reach.

Blistering, peeling, and scaling are generally localized and do not present you with the job of taking paint off an entire house. The electrical element scraping technique is quick for handling these relatively small areas. Use sandpaper to feather the edges of any localized removal, so that they will not show when you repaint.

Splintering or actual wood decay require removal of the defective material and replacement with a new board, snugly fitted into place, securely nailed, puttied, and calked. (When you replace a board, it is an excellent idea to prime it on both sides, edges, and ends before you put it in place, as part of your insurance against a repeat performance.)

HOW TO KEEP THE TROUBLE FROM RECURRING. As has been pointed out, most damage to house paint is caused by moisture. This may be water which gets into the walls from rain and snow, through cracks and crevices in the siding. It may be water from inside the house—moisture-vapor created by bathing, laundering, dishwashing. Moisture vapor, though invisible, creates tremendous pressures, passes through insulation, voids in a moisture-vapor barrier, sheathing, and siding. When it reaches an impenetrable barrier of paint film, it pushes the paint off.

To prevent this, you take one or more of the following steps:

● Reduce or eliminate moisture-vapor from within by the use of ventilating or discharge fans that take care of moisture-laden air in kitchen, bath, laundry. This is more than a painting matter; such ventilation makes a house more comfortable and healthier to live in.

● Cut off moisture from the outside by a thorough job of calking all cracks and openings through which water might enter the walls.

● Check your gutters and downspouts, to be sure they are not flooding or overflowing or otherwise adding water to the problem.

● If shrubbery is too close to the house, move it. This is a frequent problem, since small plantings are often planted what looks like a proper distance from foundations. When they grow, they turn out to be too close. It is simple to move such a planting 2 or 3 feet by digging a new hole beside it, then more or less skidding the shrub into the new position.

● Regardless of the methods from the above list you undertake, as a means of cutting down water and moisture-vapor, the most critical step is to install vents in the siding, usually beneath eaves and overhangs, so that moisture-vapor pressure cannot build up, but instead makes its way through the vents. Hardware and paint dealers sell small, round metal vents. All you do is drill through the siding at intervals all around the house and push the vents in place. Be sure, painting the house in the future, not to plug the tiny louvers of the vents with paint.

DAMAGE FROM WATER-SOAKED WOOD. Anywhere around your house that the end grain of a board butts against the side grain of another, you have a problem spot. The reason is that wood expands and contracts with changes in humidity and temperature a great deal more across the grain than with the grain. As a consequence, end-grain-to-flat-grain joints eventually open up. Water gets into the wood, soaking it, making expansion and contraction all the more violent. The paint can't keep up with all the action, and it flakes off. This type of paint failure is at its worst when vertical members, such as the sides of windows, butt horizontal members, such as sills. Or porch columns and the floor.

Preventing the recurrence of this damage is just about impossible, but you can reduce its frequency with these steps:

1. Chip and scrape away the failing paint well into the healthy area. Sand the smooth edge.

2. Making absolutely certain that the wood is bone dry (a week or more without rain) soak it with a paintable wood preservative such as Woodlife. Two soakings are better.

3. Follow with the wood primer recommended by the manufacturer of the paint you are using. If you feel the wood would soak up more primer, put on a second coat.

4. Calk the open joint. Use one of the vinyl calk materials. If they are available at your paint or hardware or building supply outlet, the calks based on acrylics are even better, since they remain flexible and are less likely to crack loose than conventional materials.

5. When the calk has hardened and cured, it's time for two coats of house paint.

THE KINDS OF DAMAGE EXCESS
MOISTURE CAUSES

Paint is peeling from this cornerboard because shrubbery too close to the house makes it impossible for the wood to get dry.

Constant source of trouble is the outside sill of windows which collect water — and also take a hard beating from hot sunlight. Notice that here the sill, the trim, and the window frame are all deteriorating, and the putty has failed. Although part of the problem here is overthick film, the basic trouble is failure to calk, prime carefully.

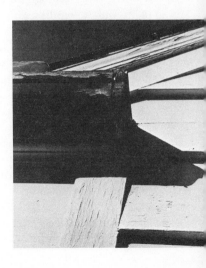

Leaking gutter lets water into the wall, making it impossible to keep paint on the house. Repair damage of this sort, even if it means replacing gutters—and stop blaming the paint.

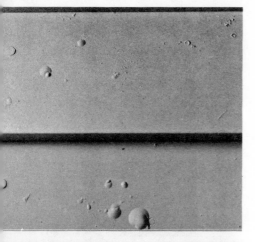

Blistering is the beginning of most water-caused paint failure. It is caused by moisture in the wood or back of the wood seeking to escape in the form of moisture vapor. When it encounters a vapor-barrier material the pressure it exerts is enough to drive the paint off the wall. The remedy is to provide relief through vents, to eliminate the source of the water, and use paints such as latex acrylics, which permit the passage of moisture vapor while blocking moisture in liquid form.

The problem with this paint failure is the lumber itself. In lower grades of beveled siding, shingles, etc., you often find boards cut with the flat grain at the surface. The flat grain is notoriously unable to hold paint, because of the differences between soft spring growth and hard summer growth. Remove such boards and replace them.

THE IMPORTANCE OF PRIMING BARE WOOD. As this book is being written, one paint manufacturer (DuPont) is on the market with a house paint which requires no primer *for purposes of adhesion,* although priming is necessary to seal soluble pigments in certain woods. By the time you read this, there may be other house paints with "the primer built in."

Nevertheless—most house paints are intended to be used over a primer. Their adhesion is less than great without the primer. Do not make the mistake of believing that you needn't bother with a primer for small areas —such as those you clean down to the bare wood making spot repairs of localized damage. Keep in mind the entire possibility that poor or improper priming may have contributed to the damage in the first place.

Every paint manufacturer produces a primer intended for his house paint. It is not always called a "primer"; Sherwin-Williams sometimes uses the term "undercoater." The purpose is the same, however. It (primer or undercoater) is designed for two functions:

1. It has tremendous adhesion to bare wood. It will often stick so tight as to foil the pressures of moisture-vapor.

2. It provides a perfect (the manufacturer's preferred choice) substrate for topcoating with the manufacturer's house paint.

As already mentioned, a wood preservative makes most woods "more paintable" than they are in their natural state. For that reason, since the spot you are working on has given indication of being a problem area, you may want to invest in extra trouble insurance by treating all bared wood with a preservative. Some preservatives not only give wood an extra affinity for finishes, but reduce the tendency of wood to shrink and swell with changing moisture conditions.

A great many homeowners have learned that latex paints are, in themselves, a sort of cure for failure due to blistering and other paint defects caused by moisture-vapor pressure. Latex paints are "waterproof," but they are not "moisture-vapor proof." In other words, the latex film will shed the water of rain and melting snow, but it will allow moisture-vapor to "breathe" through. There is no pressure back of the paint.

PREPARING SOUND PAINT FOR REPAINT. There is always a certain amount of preparation for painting, even if the substrate is entirely sound. Usually there is little work involved, but successful repaint demands that it be done. Check old paint for these conditions:

Excessive chalk. Most paints manufactured in recent years have been either "nonchalking" or "controlled chalking" and this problem is diminishing. Nevertheless, it does exist and it is serious if you are using a latex paint. The latex formulas, generally, do not "wet" the powdery residual chalk, which acts much like talcum powder in its resistance to water. Consequently, the paint doesn't stick.

Chalk is the result of weathering. The resins and binders of the old paint wear away, leaving the pigments. Normally rains wash the chalk away. This is, in fact, the principle of the so-called self-cleaning paints, since any dirt on the wall sluices away with the chalk.

There is an easy way to detect an undue amount of chalk. Wrap a double thickness of a T-shirt over your finger and rub it across the siding for a distance of about 8 inches. If the amount of chalk rubbed off by this action fills the pores of the cloth, there is too much chalk for safe painting with ordinary latex paints. What to do about it?

A hard hosing with the garden hose will often remove most of the chalk—enough to make painting safe. Check with the T-shirt trick again, when the wall is dry. An even better hose-down is possible using an "aspirator," one of those quart bottles that hold garden chemicals and fit on a garden hose, for large-scale weed spraying. Fill the bottle with a solution of 1 cup of Soilax or trisodium phosphate to a gallon of water. Then spray the house thoroughly with this solution run through the aspirator. Rinse, and the chalk should be gone. The degree of chalking and the degree of chalk sluice-down in rains are not always the same on all sides of the house. You may have to hose down only one or two sides.

There are additives for latex paints which increase their wetting action on chalk and make adhesion good. Examples are the PBL (for penetrating bonding liquid) of Dutch Boy, and a product called Emulsa-Bond.

It must be understood that excessive chalking is not a serious problem if your repaint is with an oil-base material. The foregoing information applies to latex paints, and it is important because latex paints are so rapidly replacing oil paints for every sort of household finishing.

Mildew. Mildew is one of the worst enemies of paint. It is also one of the least recognized, because it looks like ugly, splotchy gray dirt—that you can't seem to wash off. Because it is so hard to wash off, many people make the mistake of thinking it will surely hold paint. And they paint over it. The paint comes off, in big, thick, nonadhering flakes.

There is a good method of diagnosing mildew. If it won't wash off with soap and water, but it *will* wash off with a household bleach such as Clorox, it's probably mildew. And it is easy to get rid of.

Mix a solution at the rate of a cup of Soilax, a half a cup of a non-ammoniated detergent, and a quart of Clorox in a gallon of water. Swab down the house with this solution, using a push broom or some similarly large-scale method of application. Rinse.

Most modern latex paints now contain mildewcides, and the mildew growth can't feed on them. However, it *can* continue to feed on the substrate, so don't believe that a serious case of mildew can be licked merely with the use of paints calculated to kill the mildew off.

High gloss areas. Now and then you'll find areas of exterior wall, particularly under eaves, on porches, and other protected places where existing oil paints have not weathered, since they haven't been exposed to the weather. As a result, they are oily-glossy, and have an invisible accumulation of chemicals (largely calcium) which reject paint. If you attempt to paint over such a substrate, you find later that the topcoating is peeling off in large strips.

The same solutions mentioned above take care of this situation, by washing off chemicals and oils, and by etching the old paint very slightly, to provide an excellent substrate.

Just plain dirt. How dirty a house may be depends on where it is located, the presence of sulphur fumes and the like in the air, the amount of natural rainfall, and other factors. Dust accumulation is inevitable.

In the days of oil paint, the suggestion was always: carry a dusting brush in your pocket, and keep dusting ahead of yourself as you paint. Today, with latex paints which can go on as soon as the free water has evaporated—without waiting for absolute dryness—it is much easier to hose the house down to get rid of dust than to dust-brush it. Add the above-mentioned detergents in the aspirator and the washdown takes care of dust.

If you'll make a quick review of the remedies mentioned for the various malaises above, you'll find that a swab-down, hose-down is the answer to most of them, and it is never a mistake to give the house a hosing before you paint it, regardless.

Difference between flat-grain and edge-grain siding is shown here. When you buy replacement boards, be sure they look like the narrow-grained sample at the bottom.

No problem with paint here, but a piece of siding that obviously must be replaced. Carefully pull nails from the board above, then the board itself. Slide new piece up under the one above. Use nails one size larger and they'll hold in the old holes. *Photo courtesy DuPont.*

ODDS AND ENDS OF PHYSICAL REPAIRS. In addition to the replacement of boards that have begun to rot and chunks of siding that may have been mishandled at the mill, there are other little mechanical jobs that must precede a paint job.

• Nails often pop in siding, over a period of years of expansion and contraction due to the weather. Usually it is not sufficient merely to pound the nails in, because they'll pop again. Instead, carry a pocket full of nails the next *size larger*. Pull the old nails and drive in the larger. If you use galvanized or aluminum nails, and if you do not sink the heads, no puttying is necessary. However, if you drive the nail heads below the surface, it's a neater and tighter job if you putty the depressions.

• Split or cracked boards, depending on the seriousness of the damage, should be calked or replaced. Otherwise, they open up the wall to further damage from moisture.

• Examine window putty and replace any that is loose. Use a putty knife to *encourage* semiloose material to come off, so that you not only repair this year's damage, but also prevent next year's.

• Go over the entire place, looking for openings in the normal structure—places where boards have shrunk apart or settled out of juxtaposition

Speed the painting job by taking down light fixtures, mailboxes, and other things that must be painted around tediously.

It is generally easier to pull the hinge pins on storm doors and paint them in the comfort and convenience of a garage, where weather is no problem, and you can even work at night.

When shutters are well painted with a durable trim paint, you may not have to repaint them every time you paint the house — but when you do, by all means take them down and spray them. Aside from this sort of work, spraying as a means of house painting is usually messy and unsuccessful in the hands of an amateur. Drift and overspray are too difficult to control.

Bare wood is the best insurance against spot damage repeating. Scrape with a carbide-tipped scraper (top) or with a scraper-bristled brush (bottom). When the wood is bare work well into surrounding sound paint, prime carefully, spot-paint the first coat — then catch it with a second coat as you do house. *Photos courtesy DuPont.*

You save the need for replacing storm doors, screens, etc., after a few years if you keep them carefully calked and filled and painted. You can make odd-job work out of it, all the year around — with emphasis on the times when you switch seasons with screens and storms.

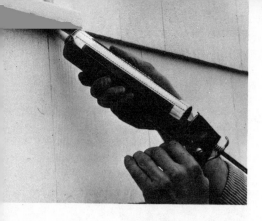

The last job before you start painting is meticulous work with a calking gun. A great deal of the bad damage shown on preceding pages could have been forestalled if cracks around window and trim had been calked. New calking materials of acrylic and other plastics last longer, protect better than old putty-like calks.

with their neighbors. In a well-constructed house, these joints were calked when the first paint job went on, but time will cause most calked joints to open. They must be recalked.

The proper way to calk. Calk is a soft, mastic material ordinarily composed of some such solids as whiting, along with a small amount of liquid. It comes bulk in cans, or more conveniently in 1-pound cartridge; which slip quickly into handy "guns." Modern calks are formulated with materials which never actually dry hard and brittle. They last longer, for that reason, since deterioration of calk is almost always due to its inability to tolerate dimensional changes in the wood or other substance it adheres to.

You must not apply calk to bare wood. If you do, absorbent wood steals the calk's volatiles, and the resulting seal is inferior. To avoid this, put a coat of primer on wood before you calk. Dab the primer into cracks and crevices, to coat as much as possible of the surfaces the calk will contact. When the primer is dry, apply the calk.

Be sure to force the material well into the openings it is filling, and allow a little extra on the surface. Then, trowel the surplus smooth with a putty knife. In inside corners, let a little "fillet" of calk remain.

Some calking materials can be painted sooner than others. Check the label for specific instructions.

Take down anything that will come off the house easily, and paint it separately. Shutters, screens, storm-door inserts and sometimes the doors themselves, mailboxes, lighting fixtures, flower boxes, and decorations are among the paraphernalia you'll find easier to paint separately. In fact, a stack of shutters in the garage makes a good project for that day it rains and you can't work on the house. Included among the things to be taken down are those you must paint *behind* for a good job.

CHAPTER ELEVEN

IS THERE A "BEST" PAINT FOR YOUR HOUSE?

LATEX PAINTS, have just about taken over the world of house painting. The advantages of latex are so overwhelming in the majority of cases that even the last of the die-hard professionals are turning to it, after years of claiming that what was good enough for their grandfathers was good enough for them. However, oil paints are not dead, and there are reasons why these materials will continue as finishes in themselves or as components of systems which may also include acrylics.

WHY LATEX PAINTS ARE SO POPULAR. Most paint manufacturers produce both acrylic latex and oil paints. Most of them prefer to sell the latex products, and promote them extravagantly, at the expense of their own oil products. The reason is an earnest seeking to gain public favor by giving people a product that is easier to use and longer lasting.

The specific advantages of latex paints are summarized in a statement by one of the world's largest manufacturers of paints, under a heading calling "latex house paint best in every way."

• Colors stay bright. Even delicate pastel colors keep their loveliness for years.

(One reason for this is the compatibility with latex vehicles of certain types of pigments that are more fadeproof. Another is the performance of the film on the house. It doesn't weather in the same manner as oil paints, and pigments are retained.)

• Cleans up with water. Brushes, rollers, and other equipment can be easily cleaned with just water.

(This is a tremendous factor, of course, since it means no paint thinners or brush cleaners to buy, and much faster cleanup than solvent-cleaning of any kind. Although the company being quoted doesn't mention it, a little soap in the water helps.)

• Paint at your leisure. Paint when there's early morning dew, paint when the sun's shining or when the surface is damp after a rain.

(It is well known, of course, that a small amount of moisture doesn't affect latex paints at all; their solvent is water, and all the moisture does is "reduce" the latex paint slightly. Of course excessive *water* on the surface would effectively thin the paint too much. It is, nevertheless, a tremendous advantage to be able to paint soon after a rain.)

• Unaffected by alkali.

(The significance of this is the excellent performance of latex paints on masonry, which often contains enough residual alkali to cause deterioration in oil paints.)

• Blister resistance. "Breathes" just enough to permit harmful water vapor to escape without breaking the paint film.

• Long-term durability. Tested for years under grueling exposure conditions all over the world.

(No paint manufacturer will tell you how long latex paints are supposed to last, because every house is a different substrate problem and every homeowner is a different painter. But acrylic paints have given indication of lasting up to six years, when applied under good conditions. Up to five years is common on typical houses in typical communities. Anything less than that is more likely to be the fault of the substrate or the painter than of the latex paint.)

• Brushes easily. Just seems to "slip on." Paint all day without any tiresome effort.

(This quality is due to the absence of a "painty stickiness." Latex paints are slippery. They brush on so easily, in fact, that there is danger of spreading each brush-load a little farther than you should for good coverage.)

• Dries lightening fast. Dry in minutes, before bugs, leaves, or anything can mar its beauty.

• No sagging or lap marks. Stop and start anywhere, anytime. Stays put and blends with the wet edge.

• Stays dazzling clean. Has a tight, slick film which sheds dirt that collects on ordinary paints.

(Latex paints are noted for the way ordinary dust and dirt sluices off them during rains.)

• Uniform soft sheen. Minimizes surface defects, accents the beauty of any home. Eliminates shiny spots under eaves.

• Fume and mildew resistance. Withstands fumes and mildew. Perfect for the "big cities" and the "Deep South."

• Brushes, rolls, or sprays. Goes on any way that will give the best-looking job quickly and easily.

• Toughness and flexibility. Stands up under punishment that completely breaks down other paints.

(Many of the breakdowns of oil paint do not occur with latex paints, because of the way the latex film will stretch and bend to accommodate movement of the substrate.)

• No staining from chalk wash. Adjoining brick and masonry surfaces will not be discolored.

(One of the shortcomings of chalking paints has always been the

Latex systems often include a complete family, from primer to topcoat, body, trim, floor. When you want a latex primer be sure it says "Latex Primer," not "Primer for Latex Paint." The latter is sometimes an oil paint and the word "latex" is misleading.

way their chalked pigments run over masonry surfaces, leaving a staining dust of pigment. This has always been a particularly bothersome problem when a painted part of the house lies over a masonry section—as a gable end of wood over a main body of brick. However, there are nonchalking or low-chalking oil paints which bypass this problem, too.)

As you can see by the foregoing claims of the manufacturer (followed by comments by the author) latex shows commanding advantages over oil paints, and there are more. . . .

Latex paints are just as good on masonry as they are on wood. When a house is made of two materials and you want to paint them both the same color, there is no need for a second paint. Color match is perfect—sheen is identical—handling and drying characteristics are the same, because it's the same paint.

Latex paints give you this same identicality of color when you paint trim and siding alike out of the same can. Corner boards, barge boards, eave lines, shutters, window casings, and many other construction members which you are painting the same color as the body of the house can be coated with regular latex house paint. As a result, they are really the same color—not just close. Few manufacturers who put out trim paints to "match" their body paints claim an exact match. There are too many differences due to sheen and texture and the visual appearance a given pigmentation may have when viewed as a velvet or a shiny surface.

Latex paints are at their best when they are used, from the bare wood up, as a "system." That is to say, if you had a brand-new, just-built, unpainted house, and if you used the preparation-primer-topcoating system recommended by any reputable manufacturer for his latex house paint, you'd have one of those "six-year jobs." However, they are just as good over previously painted houses in good condition; ordinarily a two-coat repaint job means you now have a latex house.

When a house is in bad condition, it must be made right *before you paint it with anything,* if you want a good job. Once you make it right, it's ready for latex. That is why, in so many cases, homeowners have laboriously taken the old paint off their houses: to get a clean start with latex.

One of the most welcome additions to the world of latex paints has been primers to seal the soluble pigments of cedar, redwood, philippine mahogany, or fir plywood. The latex primer may not be available in every paint line, but many paint dealers whose main line doesn't offer latex primers carry one produced by an independent manufacturer.

You'll find the primers as easy and quick to use as any other latex product . . . highly effective in sealing color . . . excellent in adhesion. Some of them are formulated with mercuric or other compounds to inhibit mildew. One of their outstanding advantages is usability over slightly damp surfaces. This means you can go to work priming bare wood an hour or so after a rain, instead of waiting the long, long time it takes bare wood to release the moisture it has absorbed. In cases of badly staining woods, you may need two coats of the latex primer, just as you'd need two coats of alkyd primer. The big difference is that the latex primer dries in an hour or so, for recoating, whether it be with another prime coat or a topcoat. The alkyd primers call for as much as two or three days of drying time—and this is enough to upset a homeowner's painting schedule.

Exterior trim is another kind of paint which is not produced by all companies in latex, although many brands are. Sometimes the label reads "Exterior Enamel," but the basic use of the material is trim. You may not find it in all colors, in latex, although it is general practice for paint companies to provide an oil-base trim paint in all the standard colors in the line.

The reason for trim paint, in the first place, is to take care of areas of a house which get an extra beating from sun and water, require extra protection, or are likely to get especially dirty and need cleaning. Constant traffic through doors inevitably means dirt from handprints, etc. This is not easy to wash off ordinary house paint, oil or latex. Around windows, the vulnerability of glass-wood joints; the inescapable exposure of sills to sun, heat, cold, and wet; and the stresses of opening and closing cause paint failures which are best resisted by a trim material.

The visible difference between trim paint and house paint is degree of gloss. Alkyd-resin oil trim paints are of a high gloss. Latex exterior enamels are a medium gloss. Both are washable and give extra protection. The latex trim paint is easier to use and includes the standard water cleanup of spills and spatters, washup of tools.

Although a great many homeowners paint their entire homes—trim and all—with latex house paints and are not displeased with performance in the trim areas, it sooner or later proves worth the slight bother of an extra can of trim paint, for the extra good job. If your dealer doesn't have a line with a latex trim component, use the oil trim, at least around doors and windows.

Porch floor paint is available in both oil and latex. Some brands are intended for either wood or concrete floors. In most cases, it takes the hard film of an oil-base floor paint to withstand the heavy traffic of a porch floor.

Metal around the house is just the same as any other surface, *once it has been primed*. Paint it with oil or latex. However, some latex paints can be put on any ordinary metal without priming, unless the metal is rusted. When there is rust, you can use a new latex metal primer—again with all the advantages of the latex system.

Masonry is best painted with latex paints. Most of the time you can use your regular house paint. Special latex paints are available, formulated particularly for masonry, although the colors are limited.

Over the years, intense research has perfected latex paints for every purpose around the house except situations plainly calling for glossy enamel. In no case are latexes substitute materials. In most cases they are best. You must have pretty strong reasons for passing up their advantages. Use them the way they are intended to be used, and they'll save you extra hours of painting time—and give you extra years of service.

PAINTS AND STAINS FOR SHAKES AND SHINGLES. If your house has a shingle or shake exterior, you handle it the same as any wood house, when you are after a solid color. If, on the other hand, you want the wood to show through the finish in the traditional manner, the product to use is a shingle stain, or perhaps a wood preservative. One difference between these materials is the amount of pigment they contain. A paint is opaque, a stain has some pigment but not enough to obscure the wood, while a preservative is clear. There is a difference, too, in the action of the materials. Paint stays on the surface of the shingles, while the stain and the preservative tend to sink in.

If your shake or shingle house is already painted, you have little choice but to continue with paint, making color changes the only difference. However, the nature of shingles is such that the preparation for repaint is usually at a minimum, and the changeover from oil paint to latex materials is at its easiest.

Shingle stains are made with a penetrating, protective liquid as the vehicle for pigments in varying amounts and in various colors. You can give just a hint of color to shakes or shingles, or you can put on enough pigmentation so that just a hint of the wood shows through. The manufacturers of cedar shingles and shakes point out that to maintain the original red-brown color, wood tone stains should be used. The wood changes color under clear penetrating materials.

Wood preservatives, used on shingles, penetrate completely into the wood, leaving no coating on the surface. They are excellent protection against mold, mildew, and decay. However, cedar is most widely used for shakes and shingles, and the wood itself is highly resistant to decay. Shakes and shingles treated with wood preservatives will take on their natural gray color, upon aging, although the action may be slower. Not all preservatives are clear, however; some of them have a color unavoidable because of their ingredients, others have some deliberate coloration. Penta-chlorophenol, phenyl-mercury-oleate, copper-naphthenate, and creosote are among the preservative materials, carried in a penetrating liquid.

Bleaches for shakes and shingles give them the silver-gray color that normally comes to cedar when it is exposed to the weather—particularly along the seacoast.

CLEAR FINISHES FOR OUTDOOR USE. There are no clear film-forming finishes for outdoor use with a life expectancy more than a year or two—and they often last a shorter time than that. The reason is, basically, the actinic and ultraviolet rays of the sun quickly destroy the quality of the film. It turns brittle, cracks, checks, flakes. Water gets through the cracks—and the only solution is to remove all the finish and start over again, preferably not with a clear finish.

To combat this early deterioration, some finish manufacturers have clear finishes which contain "ultraviolet absorbers." These are pale pigments which filter out the harmful light rays, and protect the finish. In some formulas, extra-flexible and extra-elastic resins are used. In addition, there has been some experimentation with a clear outdoor finish which weathers in the same way that house paints do. None of these materials has been developed to a point which makes clear finishes outdoors practical from the standpoint of long life.

However, only a small amount of pigmentation is required to change this picture entirely. If you like the look of wood on the outside of your house, one of the shingle stains can supply you with the answer—even though the house may not be shingled.

HOW GOOD ARE "ONE-COAT" PAINTS. Although a careful and skillful painter can work miracles with a single coat of paint, most amateurs can't. That is why a group of paints "guaranteed to cover in one coat" is of such importance to people painting their own homes. Examples are "Kem-1-Coat" by Sherwin-Williams, an oil paint, and the new one-coat latex by Sears.

The Sherwin-Williams product takes advantage of extra-opaque pigments and an extra-rich vehicle which make it easy to put on in a film thick enough to cover just about any substrate color with one coat. Special ingredients keep the thick film from wrinkling—which is almost inevitable if you overapply ordinary paints. The paint product is two or three times more expensive than most paints, but it is true that one-coat paints by any manufacturer are premium-priced. They are worth it, if you can get a satisfactory repaint job with one coat—and gain the bonus of a paint that wears longer too.

Sears calls its one-coat product "a special kind of latex house paint," with more covering power, more adhesion, more durability—up to six years instead of the four years or less of an ordinary oil paint. Most of the other features are those typical of good latex paints.

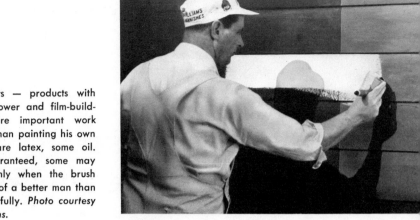

One-coat paints — products with extra hiding power and film-building ability — are important work savers for the man painting his own house. Some are latex, some oil. Some are guaranteed, some may be one-coat only when the brush is in the hands of a better man than you. Shop carefully. *Photo courtesy Sherwin-Williams.*

Typical latex house paints are not intended for one-coat use. Most manufacturers suggest two coats, for best appearance and wear. However, there is no reason why a good latex paint should not function as a one-coat, over an adequate substrate. Stop and think a moment, and you'll realize that there could never be such a thing as a paint capable of covering in one coat—*from scratch.* "One coat" has got to mean one coat over a base that is in good condition for recoat. In other words, if you paint before the existing coating has deteriorated too badly, one coat will restore it. If you are careful enough, you can even change the color with one coat. When the single coating has weathered a while, the substrate color is likely to start showing through, maybe not all over, but surely on the side of the house that takes the worst beating from the sun and rain, and surely in spots here and there where you didn't get it on quite thick enough. There's a good chance brush strokes will start to show.

Nobody will deny that the best role for one-coat paints is in a normal renewal program which involves little drastic color change. Nobody will deny that two good coats of a good house paint are better than one good coat.

Whenever the house has gone pretty far and needs painting badly, whenever you want to make a pretty serious color change, two coats of paint are impossible to beat. And with the fast-dry of latex paints, many homeowners have found they can put on two move-along coats just about as fast as they can put on one coat considering the special care necessary to apply the one-coat paints.

CHAPTER TWELVE

STEPS THAT MAKE
HOUSE PAINTING EASIER

YOU COULD buy a can of paint and a brush, get hold of a ladder and start painting. But there are some procedures that experience has indicated help make the job easier.

HOW MUCH PAINT TO BUY. Of the several common methods of computing the amount of paint a house will take, the simplest is this: Multiply the height of the eaves times the linear distance around the house. If there are wings with lower eaves, compute the body of the house and the wings separately, then add.

If the house has gable ends, add 2 feet to the height of the eaves. If it has a gambrel roof, add 4 feet to the height of the eaves.

Do not subtract for windows, unless they are very large, since the paint you save on the area occupied by windows is normally eaten up by what you need for board edges, eaves, soffets, etc.

Roof dormers typically take 100 square feet of paint.

If your house has an overhang no greater than a foot or so, ignore it. More overhang should be computed on the basis of eave line distance times overhang.

When you have the total square footage, divide it by the number of square feet per gallon given on the label of the paint. This figure varies from product to product, so check labels carefully and remember that square footages are not so much a "boast" about how far the paint will stretch as they are a warning not to stretch too far.

Trim paint is hard to figure in the above manner, since computation of square feet on the irregular shapes and surfaces of trim is just about impossible. However, a gallon of trim paint will take care of the average house. Even if 3 quarts would do it, there is little economy over buying a gallon, and you can always use the leftover paint for touching up. On the other hand, if your best guess is that a gallon won't quite do it, buy a gallon and a quart, and make a deal with the paint store to return the quart if you don't need it.

Floor paint, for porches, terraces, patios, and the like are simple enough to figure on a pure square foot basis. For odds and ends such as black wrought-iron railings, carriage lamps, etc., your guess is as good as anyone's. Remember that a little left over, stored away on a shelf in the garage, is excellent insurance against damage that should be touched up.

HOW TO BE SAFE ON A LADDER. If you happen to live in a two-story house with a gable end, you're going to be 25 feet or so in the air when you work up by the roof peak—spending a lot of time with that overhang and that attic window. Here are some tips that make a ladder safer and easier to use:

• To stand a ladder of any length up against the house, first put the foot against the house foundation. Then, starting at the other end, "walk" hand-over-hand along the rungs, raising it as you go. Do this in a quick, decisive movement, so the momentum of the ladder helps carry it erect, against the house.

• If it is an extension ladder, extend it to the desired height while it is still against the house, and easy to handle.

• Now, lift the ladder and move the base out from the foundation about one-fifth to one-quarter of the extended length. Less than that gives you an unsafe ladder so steep you'll feel insecure on it. Much more than that is likely to produce a sag and bounce in the ladder, again producing a feeling of insecurity and unsteadiness.

• To move the ladder, pull the top out from the house until it is vertical, then balance it by holding it off the ground with one hand, steadying it with the other at about head level. Step sidewise to the new position. If the ladder is a long extension, you may be better off to lower the top half before you move it.

• To take the ladder down, lower the extension and move the base in to the wall. Walk the ladder down, in the reverse of your movements raising it.

• To avoid accidents while you're on the ladder, be careful. Take the necessary precautions. If the feet don't stand evenly put a board or a brick or whatever is required under the "short" leg. When you go up:

• Be sure your shoe soles are free of slippery grass clippings, or whatever. Wear a hard-soled shoe with a heel—much safer and more comfortable than soft soles.

• Always hold on to the ladder with one hand, if possible.

• Never reach too far to either side. A good rule is, never let your hips swing outside the ladder rails.

• Never climb up a ladder beyond the point that puts the top rung below your waist.

• Plan your work for the fewest possible trips up and down the ladder.

• Never hold the paint pail in your free hand. Improvise an S hook or buy a hook from your paint dealer. You'll find it handiest if you can hang the pail outside the rail, so you won't have to reach between rungs constantly to dip the brush.

- Remember—as the man from Kansas said—"Never turn your back on a mule, or a ladder." Always face the ladder, going up and coming down. Never carry anything up or down if you can help it. A paint bucket on a light rope is easy to hoist up after you're aloft. Meanwhile, you had two hands to hold on with as you climbed.

- Above all, never extend a ladder beyond its intended length. For instance, a 24-foot ladder must have at least a 3-foot overlap. Most ladders are rigged so that you cannot extend them too far without doing it deliberately; the ropes and pulleys are attached at the proper spacing. Even for that extra couple of feet you can't reach, it's worth renting a longer ladder.

If your work is on a low wall and you can reach it from a stepladder, keep these points in mind:

- Never stand on the top step of a stepladder. If you do the chance that you'll go off balance and the ladder will scoot out from under you are too great.

- Most stepladders are sturdy and steady *only when all four* feet are hitting the ground, dividing the load between them. Use boards or other materials to build up under legs that aren't hitting the ground.

WHERE DO YOU START PAINTING FIRST? While it is pretty sensible to paint a house from the top down, most experts have special routines they follow, and most of these involve the most efficient and least laborious ladder handling, combined with the best planning for dodging the sun.

Once a ladder is set up at its full length at a gable end, you want to do all the painting you can without moving it—assuming a gable high enough to be a consideration. Thus, although you might want to establish a routine of doing the entire house body, then going back to do the trim, high on a ladder, you might decide to do them both, before you move the ladder—then have to move it back again.

The sun affects decisions of this sort, too. Suppose that there is a high gable end on your house facing due south. It is going to be too hot to paint (for your comfort and for the good of the job) from about 10:30 or so in the morning until about 3 in the afternoon. So, here's what you do:

- Set up the big ladder and work on the gable end in the morning. With latex paints and normal weather, you can be up the ladder by 8:30 or 9. Paint until the sun gets too hot.

- Switch to the east side and take care of as much of that side as you can.

- Later in the afternoon, go back up the ladder and get more done on the gable end. If you feather out the painting properly where you leave off each time, you'll be able to go back to work with never a brushmark.

Since the west side of the house gets too hot to work on in the late afternoon, you can see how easily the "sun-dodging" covered above can be translated into work on the west and the north side of the house.

When you paint the corner boards, window frames, and similar trim of a house a different color from the body, always do the body first, including the edge of the trim. Then, you have smooth sailing, putting trim paint on the flat surfaces of the trim, without the need for cutting meticulously along the edge.

The two basic brushing techniques for exterior painting are shown here. At the top, the painter uses fresh-dipped brushloads to apply paint under the edges of two or three or more boards. Then, he smooths the paint out on the flat surfaces. At the bottom, the painter uses the "three dab" method which is usually best for homeowner painters with fast-drying materials. One brush load goes under the edge. The next goes on in three or four dabs. Then — you brush out.

As you work down the ladder, be sure to feather the edge of the strip, to avoid the fat edge which might produce visible lapmarks. When you do the next strip down, you feather the new paint in, so that no lap shows.

Avoid skimping where beveled siding butts — and avoid also an overload of paint which would harden and crack. Brush up and down and crosswise over the joint, to work paint into the crack, then carefully pull out the excess paint.

First the body, then the trim. Most houses are built of beveled siding. If you'll take a look at the saw-tooth shape of things at the edge of trim, where the siding meets it, you'll understand why it makes sense to paint the body first, then the trim, even though they may be the same color. Follow these tips for handling trim and body painting:

• If you are doing a two-coat job, and the trim and the body colors are the same, put body paint on the trim for its first coat. Then switch to outdoor enamel for the second coat. This saves work and doesn't compromise quality.

• Painting body and trim differently, paint siding up to the trim, and *paint the edge of the trim with the body paint.* Carry a rag in your pocket and wipe any smears of body paint off the face of the trim, to avoid a fat edge later.

Excellent results in speed and coverage come from a variety of applicators sold by paint stores. An example is this one, in the form of a plastic handle, a plastic foam base, and a face of short-nap synthetic pile. You load it in a roller tray, top. To lay the paint on, draw the tool slowly over the surface, center. Application of a rich, uniform coat is almost automatic. Any edge works to put paint under siding or shingles, bottom. Replacement pads are available, snapping into the handle.

• Then paint the face of the trim, either immediately or later, which-ever is convenient. If you are careful, you can avoid getting any of the glossier trim paint on the body—and even if you do slop over a little, it makes little difference, compared to the bad appearance you'd have if you slopped flattish body paint over the edge of the face of the trim.

• The drying time of latex paints is so fast that you can go up a ladder, paint as much area as you can reach, working down, then go back up and second-coat the area. This cuts down tremendously on ladder moving.

• Smart painters take care of the trim and any floor involved with one entrance to the house first—say the back door. Then, when it is dry and open to traffic, they do the other entrance. That way, of course, you never paint yourself inescapably into—or out of—the house.

It is a good idea to paint porches, including the ceiling, with trim paint, to gain the benefit of its easy cleanup in areas which are likely to get dirty. Also, if you are using a semichalking paint, the chalk tends to rub off conspicuously on clothing. Trim paint doesn't rub off. It was once quite the fashion to varnish the ceilings of porches, usually because they were covered with a clear tongue-and-groove fir which was called, as a matter of fact, "ceiling." The result of such finishing is not particularly attractive—and the brightness you get from a white trim paint makes the porch more enjoyable.

APPLICATION TECHNIQUES FOR OUTSIDE WORK. The object, when you apply house paint, is to put a protective film between the weather and the material your house is made of—and to improve the ap-pearance of the building. You want the film to be complete. You want it to be thick enough for long life. You don't want it too thick, for that would encourage early cracking and fissuring. Where there are joints, you want to be sure you seal them against the weather.

Although every painter soon develops a technique of his own, most homeowners in houses with standard siding, find it easiest to put paint on uniformly, at the proper rate of spread, with the steps delineated below, and illustrated in the accompanying photographs:

1. Work in vertical units about 3 feet wide, and work one board at a time. The width may vary, painter to painter, and it may not be the same for topcoats as it is with the primers. The reason for this, as will be seen, is that the width is determined by the amount of paint you carry to the wall with each load.

2. Dip your brush the standard one-third-the-bristle-length distance. With modern latex paints, the tendency for paint to run or drip off the brush is very slight. The time-worn suggestion that you slap the brush against the side of the pail to dislodge excess may, therefore, be un-necessary. A little experimentation will tell you whether the brush slap is necessary. Remember, you want to carry as much paint with each dip as you can, without spraying the neighborhood. One way to make the load big is to avoid swinging the brush too rapidly from pail to wall.

Apply this first load of paint under the edges of the siding. It will usually cover well two under-joints across the three-foot strip you are painting.

3. Dip again. Apply this load in four dabs—two from one side of the brush, two from the other. Distribute the dabs evenly across the 3 feet.

4. Now brush out each of the dabs, blending it into its neighbor—and one of them, of course, into the edge of the preceding unit.

5. Finally, smooth the entire 3-foot strip with long, gentle strokes, using just the tips of the bristles. Watch for thick spots and blend them out. Feather the edge on the end toward the unpainted area, to make blending easier when you do the next unit.

6. Repeat the operation from the eave line to the ground—or as far down the house as your ladder will let you reach.

When you first start a unit in this manner, adjust the width to match the amount of paint you bring up with each load in relation to the way the siding is taking the paint—plus the degree of thickness you are after. You may find that the four-dab method, with *your* method of dipping, *your* selection of paint, and *your* degree of brush-out may let you go 3½ feet—or may hold you to 30 inches. (*Remember:* do not overspread, as the easy brushing of modern paints may lead you to do.) It is almost certain, as you do second coats or topcoats over primer, that the coverage will be different. This is good, because it means the units will not coincide exactly, and will not have the blended edges, unit to unit, all in the same place. Should it happen that your units are the same width, deliberately vary them, to avoid exact juxtaposition of edges.

Using this method of painting on high walls, with a well extended ladder, you work from right to left, unless you are a lefthanded painter. Paint from the top down as far as you can reach—until the slope of the ladder takes you too far from the building. Then move the ladder 3 feet to the left. This is easy to do by shoving it away from the wall at the top, tilting it about 18 inches, and letting it come back against the house. Then, move the base over 3 feet, again making the ladder straight.

If you did your preparation properly, there are not wide cracks in the house's skin, because you calked them all. There may be, however, relatively small cracks, not worth the bother of calking since the paint should fill them. To be sure it does, "cross-brush" all cracks. This means brushing across the crack, to squeegee paint into the opening, then brushing with the crack to make it smooth. In the case of butted siding joints, you need a third brushing. First, you brush across the crack. Then you make a vertical cross-board stroke. This, of course, gives you brushmarks in the wrong direction. So you smooth, finally, with another light stroke across the crack. There is almost always a preferred direction for this stroke, determined by the height of the siding on either side of the crack—a direction that will not scrape off a thick load of paint.

BRUSH HANDLING WITH LATEX PAINTS. Because latex paints dry so fast, there is a chance that they may start to harden up around

Another version of the "non-brush" applicator is a scrub-brushlike model, useful on siding but especially on shakes or shingles. One row of bristles is separated from the others, for use under edges.

the heel of the brush, while you're working, particularly when the weather is hot and dry. Professional painters often use two brushes to overcome this problem. When a brush starts to load up, they stick it in a pail of water to soften. When the second brush begins to accumulate paint at the heel, they quick-wash the first, put the second in the pail, and continue their work with the first brush.

You can adopt the two-brush system—or you can make the best of it with one brush by *carefully scraping off the accumulation around the heel* as often as necessary. Then, after a couple or three hours of painting, wash out the brush, shake it as dry as possible, and continue. When the weather is hot, the colder the rinse-water the better.

FINE WORK ON OUTDOOR TRIM. The same sash tool you used for trim work indoors (see Chapter 6) works for windows and screens outdoors, and the same technique of working from the inside out applies. Again, you'll lower the top sash and raise the bottom sash, in order to handle surfaces not normally exposed. As with inside doors, paint panels, then cross members, then stiles—working from the inside out.

No surface of any house takes any worse beating than the window sills and the lower puttied edges of windows on the south side of the house—unless it might be the same places on the west side of the house. To forestall trouble on these surfaces, use all the precautions you've read about—times two. When there is fissuring or cracking, scrape clean. Use a wood preservative. Prime carefully. Topcoat with two or three thin coats, rather than one thick coat. Lean toward the extra water-resistance of glossy materials. Give every coat adequate drying time, but don't let any undercoat dry too long, or adhesion may not be at its best.

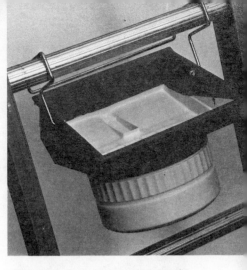

Proper technique for painting shakes and other rough-sawn materials is to move brush or applicator in the direction of the texture. Shake painter, shown here, is an example of foam-and-pile tools that are excellent for exterior work.

Tremendous worksaver for people who like to roll paint on outside is a plastic tray that screws on top of a special plastic pail, half-gallon capacity. When you tilt the tray, paint comes up through a "well," recharging the tray. Saves countless trips on the ladder.

It is worth mentioning again: ordinary house paint is plenty of protection of such non-critical areas of trim as the corner boards, barge boards, eave lines, and flat trim around windows. Sashes, muntins, mullions, and doors are best painted with a specific trim paint—be it latex exterior enamel or alkyd—in order to insure the maximum protection and resistance to weathering.

Although lap marks are a thing of the past with latex paints carefully feathered and blended, it is always wisest to end up a day's work with a complete wall—or at some such natural break as a door's edge, the setback of an overhang, or other places where the ending and the beginning are least likely to show.

HOW THE ONE-SIDE-A-YEAR PROGRAM WORKS. Since your house paint does not deteriorate at the same rate on all four exposures, you have available a painting program much appreciated among homeowners for the way it spreads out the work.

Under average conditions, the southern exposure of a house weathers fastest. The sun is more constant and hottest. The western exposure weathers next fastest. Then east. Then north; in fact, northern weathering is often extremely slow. Suppose, just for discussion, the paint you put on the house has a five year life. If you painted your home carefully and well, it would be five years before it would need painting again. But, due to variables in weathering, the whole house wouldn't need it. Just the fastest-weathering side would be ready for paint.

Suppose, when that southern exposure indicated the need for repaint, you were to do the whole house? You would be building more film thickness than you need on the west side, even more on the east, and a lot more on the north. To avoid this, and to spread the painting out over

Make painting as easy on yourself as possible by such things as a special wide-mouth pail, with a hook for the ladder rung. Big feature here is a piece of coathanger wire across the pail, through two nail-punched holes. You rest the brush on the wire — and you use the wire as a means of getting surplus paint off your brush without having it run down the side of the pail.

as long a period as possible, there is the one-side-a-year program:

Start with a well-painted house. For the first four or five years, keep a close check for premature spot failure. Repair such failure and correct the causes for it.

At the end of four years, or five, or six, when the south side begins to show the need for it, paint that side—and that side only—using only one coat, carefully applied. A quick and simple job.

Next year, do the west side, one coat.

The third year, put a careful one coat on the east side.

The fourth year, the north side. (Watch the north side most carefully for mildew and other contamination, owing to the length of time it has been exposed.)

Depending on the paint you are using, the degree of weathering, and the thickness of your application, you may get a year off at this point. Maybe two. But, when the fail-first side of the house barely begins to show the need for more paint, start the cycle again.

Painting one exposure of a house is a fairly tolerable amount of painting—not enough to turn a man against homeowning. Meanwhile, the one-side-a-year program is virtual insurance against the amount of overbuild that might result in failure due to too much paint on the house.

CHAPTER THIRTEEN

PAINTING MASONRY AND METAL

MUCH MASONRY—such as careful brickwork—is far too beautiful to be painted, since its charm comes from the patterns of brick and mortar. Much other masonry is strictly functional in purpose and can be improved with a coat of paint which may change the way it reflects light, may make it easier to keep clean, may protect it from damage, or may just make it look better. In fact, you get a little tired of the monotonous gray of concrete and concrete blocks, and giving color to concrete has become a welcome brightener around many a home.

Thus, you are eager to paint the basement walls white, to make a downstairs activity room brighter. Weary of the way a retaining wall along a driveway may dominate the scene, you paint it green and it disappears. Concrete front steps, a pretty dull and lifeless greeting for visitors, brighten with paint; steps in another area become safer in dim light when you paint treads and risers two different colors. A panel of bricks in one wall of a house that seemed like a nice decorative trick at one time blend into the rest of the building under a coat of paint. With the promise of color instead of gray, you step into the project of a decorative masonry-block wall as a privacy screen along one side of the terrace.

Painting masonry is not difficult—in fact it may be easier than painting the wooden parts of a house. Preparation, made to sound ominous in much material you read about the subject, is often simpler than getting wood ready to paint. The very nature of cementitious products makes them less trouble than calk; patching is easy. Old finishes which may have to come off can be attacked with more rigorous methods than you'd dare use on wood.

You may not, however, put any paint on masonry. There are certain prescribed types. This needn't be any kind of a deterrent, for one of the best is plain latex house paint for outdoors, wall paint for indoors.

THE PROBLEM OF ALKALI. New concrete and mortar are very alkaline in nature, and ordinary paints cannot survive, applied over alkali. One reason why is that the oils may combine with the alkali to make a form of soap—which is not weather resistant. Flaking and peeling—even chalky disintegration—are almost inevitable. As masonry ages, the alkali leeches away until in time there may be none on the surface. Water will bring a certain amount of alkali to the surface, however. When masonry is more than two years old—and when it is dry—ordinary paints give service. But—why take the chance? There are several varieties of alkali-resistant paints readily available, and easy to use:

• Latex paints, including house paints, but also including latexes specifically formulated for concrete. Most paint dealers carry one or more of several nationally distributed brands, and many major paint manufacturers include a latex masonry paint. *Not all water-thinned* paints are appropriate for use on masonry. Do not use them unless the label specifies masonry as a recommended use. Virtually any color is available, and color retention is excellent.

• Portland cement paints come in powder form, to be mixed with water. They have been used for a long time with good results, but they present certain problems in application. First of all, they are not meant to dry, but rather to harden or set much in the same manner as concrete or mortar set. To make sure this happens, and that the mixture doesn't merely dry up and dust off, portland cement paints must be applied to damp surfaces, and must be kept damp for as long as seventy-two hours, so the cement in the paint can cure. These paints are generally economical. Pastel colors are sometimes available, and deeper shades are possible with powdered pigments. One thing to remember if you are thinking of using a portland cement paint is that it establishes a substrate over which other types of paint can't be used without special surface conditioners. Despite the rugged sound of "portland cement paint" as a name, these coatings are rather delicate.

• Oil-base stucco paints are similar to oil-base house paints except for the addition of ingredients intended to increase resistance to alkali. They are acceptable for use on very old masonry, with the risk that water may bring alkalis to the surface in quantities great enough to override their alkali-resistant properties.

• Rubber-base paints utilize synthetic rubber solids, and are excellent in resistance to alkali. Wear and abrasion resistance make them the top choice for basements and porch floors, swimming pools, steps, walks, patios.

There are a few other masonry coatings of little interest to the home-owner—and in fact not readily available to him. These include catalyzed coatings, air-curing urethanes, and single-container epoxies, all of which are expensive and difficult to use. Asphalt or bituminous coatings are included among masonry paints, but their purpose is generally to waterproof masonry in direct contact with the soil, and as such are not really paints.

PREPARING THE SURFACE FOR PAINT. To begin with, you should never consider painting masonry until it is at least a month or six weeks old. If possible, delay painting new concrete for six months. This allows the weather to clean the surface, washing away release agents which may have been used to coat forms, and giving the surface a chance to free itself of nonhardened materials—that is, cement and sand which may not have retained moisture long enough to cure completely. This, of course, is unlikely to be a condition on bricks or concrete blocks—but it might be on the mortar.

Use a wire brush or a very stiff bristle brush to remove loose dirt, masonry particles, and other material which might interfere with the smoothness of the paint or with its adhesion. Hose down the wall with a hard stream of water, to sluice down loosened dirt. Check for oily or greasy areas, and wash them with a strong solution of trisodium phosphate or Soilax or a similar cleaning product. Rinse thoroughly.

Efflorescence is the name given to a saltlike, whitish, powdery material which gathers on the surface of masonry. It is caused by water dissolving salts in the masonry. The water then carries the salts to the surface where they dry—and often defy all ordinary means of removing them. Since paints do not stick to efflorescence, it must be removed chemically, if necessary. Mix one part of muriatic acid in three parts of water, always adding the acid to the water—never the reverse—and always pouring it slowly. Protect your eyes. Wear rubber gloves. Swab this acid on the efflorescence to dissolve it, then rinse thoroughly. Since more moisture will most likely bring more efflorescence to the surface, paint as soon as possible.

Most masonry paints are latex formulas, and their water may be absorbed too rapidly by dry masonry. For that reason, the first step with latex masonry paints is to hose down the surface, to reduce absorbency. As soon as free water has drained off, you can paint.

Sometimes such concrete surfaces as steps, patios, and porches are quite smooth and hard, the result of steel troweling a little too much. Paints have a tough time adhering to such surfaces, but the same muriatic acid bath mentioned above etches a little "tooth" into the smooth concrete, and adhesion is again good. Be sure to rinse thoroughly.

Previously painted masonry. Painted masonry, like painted wood, can mean no problems whatsoever, if the paint is in sound condition. Be sure it's clean, and paint over it. Old paint in poor condition, however, may require some work. If the paint is flaking or peeling there is little sense trying to paint over it. It is almost certain to continue peeling—and taking your new paint off with it. The best solution—in fact the only solution in the opinion of many experts—is sandblasting. This removes the old paint, and to a degree it removes the reason for the failure of the old paint. Sandblasting is never so complicated a job that a fairly handy homeowner couldn't do the job, but the equipment involved is complex and renting it is not often easy. Although a power wire brushing does a fair job, it's better to check the classified pages for a sandblasting contractor.

Sometimes a finish that looks sound enough is entirely unsuited for painting. Examples are calcimine and whitewash. They must be removed. Calcimine is fairly easy to get off, using a stiff brush and detergent and warm water. Whitewash may require sandblasting, however.

A masonry conditioner is the best safeguard against failure, too, when old paint is chalking and dusty. It tightens up the loose surface and provides a good substrate for any topcoat. Another method of sealing up a chalky, dusty substrate is with additives for regular masonry paint, similar in their action to the additives used to improve adhesion of latex house paints to chalky old paint. The practice is, generally, to add a quart of the modifying material. There is no change in the handling of the masonry paint, except that drying time is usually doubled.

These additives are frequently recommended for latex paint to be used on *asbestos siding or shingles.*

After an old finish has been removed from masonry, the surface is usually dusty and somewhat soft, and requires a prime coat of "masonry conditioner" such as DuPont 919 Masonry Surface Conditioner. The purpose of these coatings is to seal and harden the virgin surface.

One more precaution regarding masonry painting, if you are using a latex material: there is often unsuspected steel or iron in concrete—left from form nails, or from impurities in the concrete or mortar mixture. These are often difficult to spot unless they rust, and that is one reason why it is best to give concrete a few months to reveal all its possible problems before you paint. Rust will pinpoint metal for you after a few rains, and you can doctor the problem in advance with a metal primer. Otherwise, rust will bleed through latex materials.

When the masonry is rough and porous. Sometimes masonry you want to paint is rough and textured (particularly certain types of concrete blocks) and would be difficult to paint. Not only would the deep pores be hard to work the color into, but also filling them would use gallons of extra paint. If you run into this situation, mix a batter-thick slurry of cement and water and give the surface a first coat with this material. If the porosity is extreme, you may even need a little very fine sand in the slurry. Brush it on with a whitewash brush, working it into the pores of the masonry. *Important:* This slurry, being cementitious, should be applied to predampened masonry, and must be kept from drying out for two or three days, the same as portland cement paints.

Paint stores and building supply dealers often sell a prepackaged mixture in powder form, ready to be mixed with water to do this job. Some of these products (Thoro-Seal is an example) serve the additional function of making the wall more watertight. Also, in the lines of some paint manufacturers there are special masonry primers which contain filling materials. An example is Primafil, made by Pratt & Lambert.

Patching cracks and loose mortar. Cracks in masonry and in mortar joints, and loose mortar must be filled before you paint, not only for the sake of appearance, but to make the job weather tight. This job is easier, in many ways, than the calking you do on wood. Here are the steps:

1. Chip and dig away all loose material along a crack or along mortar joints. Use a chipping chisel, a screwdriver, a nail—anything that will help you remove all unsound masonry.

2. Using dry-bagged ready-mixed "sand-mix" concrete, stir up a batch of good stiff consistency, using only enough water to make the material pliable.

3. Thoroughly dampen the crack. Let it drain or dry until there is no free-standing water.

4. Trowel in the concrete mix, pressing it firmly, to make sure it fills the crack, without voids.

5. Keep the patch damp for at least 48 hours—longer if your schedule permits.

6. For an extra sound job, to insure against the chance that the patch might not bond to the walls of the crack, paint on a mixture of "neat cement and water"—with no sand. Make the material of good brushing consistency. Dampen the crack first, then be sure to cover all surfaces with the neat cement slurry. Apply the patching material before the slurry dries.

Remember: This patch is now *new concrete,* regardless of the age of the masonry itself. It must be allowed at least two weeks to cure and set and rid itself of excessive alkali. Even then, it is best to use only a latex paint, to avoid failure of the paint over the patch.

Many paint stores and masonry supply houses carry special patching materials which utilize special latex liquids. An example is Sherwin-Williams' Loxon Latex Concrete. These materials provide extra strong adhesion, excellent paintability, and ease of use. There are, also, proprietary "conditioners" to be added to regular cement-water patching mixes, to increase their adhesion and to insure good curing, even in small quantities.

APPLICATION TECHNIQUES FOR MASONRY PAINT. All of the masonry finishes except portland cement paint can be applied with a roller, and this is often the best way to do it. Use a large roller with long nap, so you can be sure to work the paint into the textures of the masonry.

If you prefer a brush, use a fairly large whitewash brush, in the interest of speed, and because masonry will wear out a fine brush rather quickly.

When you paint floors, porches, walks, and other concrete on the flat, the fast way to do it is to pour a pint or so on the surface, then roll it out. With a little practice you'll be able to blend successive patches together into a smooth, continuous coating. Floors, terraces, and the like, should always have two coats or more at the first painting, since they wear through too soon under traffic unless a fairly thick coating is built up coat by coat. After the initial painting, you can keep such floors in good shape by watching for wear-through, spot patching the areas that go bad earliest, and doing the whole floor every two or three years.

Some concrete floors may be dangerously slippery underfoot. You can make them skidproof by adding a small amount of very fine sand to one of the more heavy-bodied outdoor paints. Ask your paint dealer about antiskid paints he carries. Generally, the rubber-base coatings have a naturally high coefficient of friction, and should be considered when slipperiness is a factor.

A roller with a nap half an inch or longer gives the fastest work on masonry. Roll slowly, so the nap can work into depressions and give you a clean, smooth color. When painting a flat surface, pour paint and roll it out.

Since masonry is textured, it takes more paint than smooth wood surfaces. This suggests working out of a bigger pail, and more broadside methods. Paint stores sell a grid which hangs on a 5-gallon pail, giving you plenty of paint with a minimum of dripping. Use an extension handle for large areas and high walls, to save legwork.

ABOVE GRADE, ON GRADE, BELOW GRADE. Some masonry paints carry label specifications as to where they are most satisfactory, as regards grade level. To appraise such paints for your use, use these working definitions:

Above grade means masonry above ground, on both sides, thus not exposed to constant moisture from the earth.

On grade means masonry in contact with the earth, such as a concrete slab poured on the ground.

An area of masonry often left unpainted which contributes to a better looking home is the foundation wall below the siding. A latex house paint works as well on concrete or block foundation as it does on shingles, shakes, or siding. As a result, you can lower your house and make it more compatible with the earth by painting ugly masonry.

Below grade means masonry in contact with the earth on one side, such as a basement wall.

These conditions are of concern because of the transmission of moisture-vapor through masonry. A floor poured on grade may seem to be quite dry; actually it is transmitting moisture constantly from the damp earth below. The same is true of below-grade walls and floors, of course, and the result is a pretty touchy substrate. It is standard practice to pour concrete on a moisture-barring film, and to coat the earth side of below-grade with a heavy coating of asphalt, to minimize or even eliminate the moisture-vapor problem. Nevertheless, since you cannot always know what moisture transmission there may be, and since any barrier lets some vapor through, you must select paints for use on or below grade which allow the vapor to "breath." This means, in fairly general order of preference: latex portland cement, and rubber-base for walls, and it means latex patio-floor-pool enamel, rubber-based floor and deck enamels or urethane floor paints for floors, decks, porches and the like.

One of the remarkable characteristics of latex patio-floor-pool enamel is that some brands can be used on blacktop or asphalt surfaces.

PAINTING METAL AROUND THE HOUSE. In no phase of painting around the house do manufacturers set down such hard-and-fast guidelines for their own products as they do in metal painting. All of them have set up procedures for metal preparation, priming, and topcoating which they feel safe in recommending, even though painting metal is a touchy business. That is why you are wisest when you follow, as closely as you can, the recommendations of the *manufacturer of your selected topcoat*.

This will involve, typically, a careful reading of the topcoat label, to find out what primer—if any—is recommended. Then, buy that primer and read its label carefully, to find out exactly how it is to be used. Pay attention when you paint metals, because a lot of the lenience disappears. A wide variety of things work on wood. Not so with metals.

When you set out to put a finish on metals, you must first take into account the way all metals *oxidize*. In common metals, like steel and iron, this means simply rust, but it happens in less conspicuous ways with all metals.

You use a primer on metals to combat or circumvent this oxidation. Some primers contain chemicals which neutralize the acid condition which is, in most cases, a prerequisite of rust and corrosion. In other instances, the function of the primer is to block out moisture and oxygen, both of which must come into contact with the metal before it can oxidize. Whichever of these basic functions is primarily in the primer recommended, it has another purpose: it provides a perfect substrate for following coats. In other words, primers stick to metal, and paint sticks to primers.

The miracle of latex paints reaches into metal finishing in ways that at least equal their remarkable performance on wood. Many manufacturers put out a latex paint which, in itself, is a good metal primer. Put the house paint, they say, on aluminum or galvanized iron without a second thought, if the metal is clean and not rusted. Other paint makers ask you to use one of their primers, to be sure their topcoats have optimum substrate conditions. Again: read the labels.

Getting the metal ready to paint. Each of the various metals used around the house has its own requirements, insofar as preparation is concerned.

Steel and iron must be free of loose rust to be ready for priming with typical red-lead formulas—or more conveniently with one of the new latex metal primers that is ready for recoat in thirty minutes. Several manufacturers have this type of primer, including Colorizer and DuPont.

Galvanized iron, the material of most gutters and downspouts, will take most latex paints without priming, if it is clean and free from oil. New galvanized iron usually has an oil coating, left over from the manufacturing processes. In a few months, this oil will weather away. You can remove it for earlier painting with paint thinner or a dishwashing detergent in warm water. Zinc-chloride primers are sometimes recommended for galvanized metal. Check labels to see if the manufacturer of the latex paint you have selected approves the use of his paint right on clean galvanized, or whether he wants a primer used.

Rusted galvanized iron is no longer galvanized, and must be treated as plain steel. If you wire-brush the loose rust off and give it one or preferably two coats of a fast-dry latex primer, it is ready for topcoating.

Aluminum doesn't rust, of course, but it does show the effects of corrosion in the form of a white powdery substance. It is easy to remove with a wire brush or detergent and water. Clean aluminum takes latex paints, or some systems may call for zinc-chloride priming. Follow the manufacturers' recommendations.

Copper sometimes takes on a greenish deposit—the equivalent of rust. Use fine sandpaper to get rid of it. You'll get best results if you use a fast-dry latex primer.

Since it is the purpose of primers to inhibit rust and other corrosion, *quantity counts*. Do not brush any primer out too much. Use two coats for the greatest protection. Although some metal primers have a fairly long life without topcoating, they are not intended for prolonged exposure to the weather. Get the finished coating on as soon as possible.

Proprietary primers. Several manufacturers of chemical coatings produce primers of excellent quality, although the companies may not, in themselves, be widely known as manufacturers of topcoatings. Derusto and Rustoleum are two well-known names in this field. Both are specialists in metal finishing and your dealer may recommend them to you.

Remember, that rust and corrosion cannot take place except when moisture and oxygen are present. So—once you have properly prepared metal for painting and primed it if required, be sure the topcoating you give it does its share in shielding the metal from water and air.

Part II
WALLPAPERING

CHAPTER FOURTEEN

THE ROLE OF WALLPAPER IN HOME DECORATING

A HOME WOULD be pretty monotonous if every room were painted, if no room had the special interest that the patterns and textures wallpaper alone can give. On the other hand, a home would be rather giddy if every wall in every room blossomed with the colors and patterns many wallpaper books present. That is why the best use of wallpaper is in *some* rooms and often on only one or two walls of those rooms. The decision as to which rooms and which walls may be strictly a matter of personal likes and dislikes, or it may depend on decorative factors. For example, there is a saying among interior decorators that "The furnishings of a room take care of the first 3 feet up from the floor—but above that height the way the walls are handled make or break the room."

On that upper 5 feet or so, paint and paper and even wood paneling and masonry must supply the balance that makes a room full of furniture a good room or a bad one.

It is not difficult to utilize this basic decorating truth in your own selections. Here are some guidelines:

• Rooms in which you spend relatively little time can stand more pattern than rooms you are in for longer periods. Thus a bedroom is often a better candidate for wallpaper than a living room.

• Rooms filled with physical activity are less likely candidates for patterned walls than rooms of quiet dignity. For example, a game room might become frenetic with a busy wallpaper pattern, while a pattern might fit in quite well with the goings on in a study.

• Rooms with considerable natural decoration—such as windows, shelves of books, a big fireplace wall, etc.—are often better with plain walls than patterned.

• In a room where the furniture itself establishes a good variety, plain walls are often best. For example, the table, the several chairs, the china closet or hutch cabinet, and hanging chandelier of a dining room may be enough decor, without the need for patterned walls.

• When you have a collection of wall decorations such as pictures, prints, hanging, knick-knack shelves, etc., the walls are usually well enough taken care of without pattern of their own.

127

Of course, pattern vs. plain does not always indicate paper vs. paint. The difference and the choice may be between a strikingly patterned paper and one that is subtle—or even virtually plain.

Many of the visual illusions mentioned in the chapter on color (Chapter 8) are the properties of pattern as well. Patterned walls make a room seem smaller. Vertical stripes make a ceiling look higher and horizontal patterns make it seem lower. Patterns can make a hallway narrow. They can bring closer the far end of a long, narrow room. And like color, they can provide a highlight background for a special grouping of furniture.

WALLPAPER AND FURNITURE STYLE. Although the selection of papers or other wall coverings for your home is a matter of personal taste, various styles of furniture are best accompanied by certain patterns and styles of wallpaper. Any well-staffed wallpaper store has personnel qualified to help you adapt paper to furnishings, but these suggestions will help in the selections:

• Colonial and Early American furniture calls for wallpaper patterns copied from papers found in old homes—and sometimes as linings in drawers and chests. There are, in most wallpaper catalogs, good adaptations

Traditional furniture, such as this Colonial setting, can be augmented by wallpaper designed specifically for the period and the style. Yet, it need not be purely traditional in itself. This eagle and star pattern has a fresh, modern feeling, even though its design elements are Early American.

Decorating Retailer

of Early American motifs which, though not authentically "antique," do provide excellent settings for the maple and pine of Colonial furniture design. The colors of Early American are most often the simple blues, greens, ochres, and reds that are often called "earth colors."

• Georgian styles, including Chippendale, Heppelwhite, Sheraton, and some of the more elegant Colonial American designs such as Goddard, Savery, and early Duncan Phyfe. Wallpapers with floral prints as well as geometric designs were traditional with such furniture. The furniture designers often acted as decorators, too, specifying the papers, colors, and arrangements. There was considerable use of pictorial papers, as well as "running" patterns repeating the curves and shapes of the furniture designs.

• Louis styles—XIV, XV and XVI—were symbolic of 18th century France where they originated. Somewhat florid in design motif, they were more ornate than British cabinetwork across the Channel, although Louis XVI was somewhat calmer. There was a nationalistic feeling in wallpapers used in rooms filled with Louis designs. The fleur-de-lis, national flower of France, was often used. At the same time fat little angels crept into designs —"cherubim." Elegant country scenes, historic events, brocade and damask patterns were frequent. The general character of French decoration was set almost entirely by the royalty, toned down somewhat in French Provincial, but still observing the same decorating motifs.

• American Provincial, as decorators sometimes call the primitive, homemade furniture of the 18th and early 19th centuries which is so much admired and copied these days, requires paper that is "homemade," too. Rural Americans often made simple symmetric stencils to put painted designs directly on the wall. Excellent reproductions of such stencils are available in wallpapers. Other wallpapers, such as those suitable with Colonial furniture, go well with Primitive American, too, but it is never a good idea to use anything very complicated or ornate with this simple furniture, or the result may be the look of the country girl visiting her rich city cousin.

• Modern furniture is unfettered in design. Anything goes, and often too much does. Textures, grasscloths, tweedy patterns, geometrics, stripes, abstract designs, even Oriental motifs all go with modern. The range is complete from dignity to absurdity, and you pick the pattern you like. Remember, however, the inevitable change in the most current ideas in modern. You can paper a room in a Georgian pattern and still be correct ten years later. A modern design may be "last year's wallpaper" by the time the snow falls.

• Children's furniture and the young, happy nature of the nursery or young child's room have inspired a number of gay wallpaper patterns. Although these are usually designed to meet the parents' idea of what a child might like to have on his walls, many of them actually carry the kinds of designs and colors which help make a nursery a more child-oriented room. Toys, animals, alphabets and numbers, simple shapes, and bright colors are among those most often used in children's rooms.

Availability of fabrics that precisely match papers present an excellent example of decorating unity. Pillow and mattress cover in this girl's room display the same floral pattern. A good wall treatment idea is the use of a complementing paper, as on the wall behind the model. The patterned paper continues as a cornice or border over the plainer paper, cut out with scissors along the pattern line.

SOME EFFECTIVE WAYS TO USE WALLPAPER. When you think of wallpaper for a room, you needn't necessarily think of it for all four walls, or even for *all* of any individual wall. It is very common practice to combine paint and paper, a plain paper with a patterned paper, and paper with paneling.

Whenever good stylists in home decoration work out combinations of paper with other materials there are always good and sufficient reasons, however. It is never done just out of whimsy, unless the whimsy happens to be backed by good taste and good sense. As with any other phase of home design, the reasons for mixing paper with other materials in a *traditional* setting must be based on good use of the traditional design elements. You like period design, and for that reason, you follow all the requirements that tradition has established.

When a home is modern—truly modern, that is, and not merely the same old shapes and room divisions with clamshell trim instead of ogee moldings—the rules are different, because there are no rules. The interesting and uncommon shapes that result from single-pitch roofs, for example,

Wallpaper doesn't have to do the entire job. Rough stained boards on the papered wall help make a compatible modern setting for traditional furniture in this room. Notice that the wall which is already decorated with draperies is simply painted.

welcome new approaches to the use of materials, and a wall might be composed of brick, paneling, and wallpaper in a combination quite as satisfying as a pure Georgian paper back of a pure Georgian chest on chest.

Start thinking about wallpaper with a consideration of the amount of paper the room *needs* for maximum attractiveness, and the amount of work involved in papering vs. painting or other wall treatment. As an example, visualize a living room in the corner of the house, with a window on one wall, three windows on the other wall, and a door on a third wall. To begin with, that wall with three windows is pretty well decorated as it stands. Perhaps you'd want to drape all three windows into a unit, with a cornice or some other treatment. Even if you curtain them individually, there is a lot going on. Besides, it is not the easiest job in the world to hang wallpaper around windows, or to plan the arrangement of a wallpaper pattern so that all three windows look right. That, of course, casts a lot of votes for painting that wall. How about white? Or the off-white that is the background color of your wallpaper? That way, you'd make the wall light in appearance, despite its position on what must be the darkest side of the room.

It wouldn't be too much bother to work around the single window on that one wall, or around the door. And the plain wall is straightaway wallpapering. So, you might decide to hang paper on three walls and paint the fourth. However, your furniture might be such that you can handle the wall with one window, and also the one with the door, in a way that would make them attractive. If so, why not paper that one big wall?

Three different wallpapering tricks are used in this modern setting. The main room is papered in a small, almost invisible check. The alcove with dressing table has a modern floral. Over the bed, flower groupings cut from the floral pattern are spotted informally.

Suppose the situation is a nursery where children spend a lot of time and imprint their frequently untidy hands on the wall with certain regularity. You do want the brightness and pattern and interest of a good nursery paper, but the problems of keeping paper clean are a factor. There are lots of good, washable papers, but they are rarely as washable as a good semigloss enamel. Why not nail up a simple "chair rail" about 30 inches from the floor. Paint the chair rail and the wall beneath it one of the good, happy colors from the wallpaper, and put the wallpaper above the chair rail. You cut down on maintenance work, and you end up with a very attractive room. Keep in mind, if you like this idea, that *latex* paints go well over old wallpaper; you don't have to go through any extra preparation for the painted part of the wall if you happen to be working in a room that has been papered.

Here are some applications of the principles suggested in the preceding paragraphs:

• Use the chair rail or wainscot idea in hallways, to keep the lower half of the walls washable, but give the area some character. This is particularly good in the heavy-traffic area at the head of a stairway, where a landing may lead off into two or more hallways.

• Reverse the wainscot idea as a means of "lowering" a ceiling that is too high. Nail up a picture molding a foot or so down from the ceiling, all around the room. Carry the ceiling paint color down the walls to and including the molding. Paper the walls below the molding. The visual effect is that of a ceiling only as high as the line where wallpaper and paint meet.

• Use wallpaper to provide interest in a front entrance, where there isn't very much appropriate furniture.

Mural papers—gigantic maps or pictorials—help establish the mood of a room, and are often used on large, plain walls, on balconies in split levels, and in family activity rooms.

Special papers for bathrooms may be completely waterproof, scrubbable, and immune to steam damage. The selection here was a tilelike pattern to complement the tile atmosphere of the bath, but an endless variety of patterns is available, and with them you can take away some of the clinical feeling many bathrooms have.

• Put wallpaper in the back of open shelves, to tie them into the rest of the room, unless such shelves are used for the display of knick-knacks and the pattern of the paper might distract from the objects on view.

In a house that's modern—or a household that likes modern and offbeat ideas, regardless of the architecture—you can take the lid off completely with wallpaper ideas.

• Paper three walls with a floral pattern, and do the fourth in stripes.

• Run stripes up one wall, across the ceiling, and down the other— but be prepared to accept the consequences. (Papering a ceiling is difficult, however, and not really a job for homeowners to do themselves.)

• Use a wallpaper in wilder colors that you'd dare try with paints, because the pattern of a paper helps make the color more acceptable. Combine colors with white woodwork and trim—or with other strong colors that are compatible.

• If you are in search of the truly novel wall, examine a few patterns with the idea of hanging them horizontally, instead of vertically. (You start at the ceiling and work down.)

• Never overlook the possibility of using identical patterns in paper and draperies, but remember that you may get the best effect doing this if you put a plain background color on the wall with the draperies, so that there will not be a misfitting of the patterns.

Wallpaper doesn't have to be confined to walls. There are many methods of using it to increase decorative interest and to unify the various elements of a room.

• Put wallpaper on a flush door—or a pair of flush sliding doors in a bedroom. If you paint the casings the background color of the paper, this method of door handling will cut down on the degree to which the door breaks up the wall.

• Do the opposite: make a door more of a feature, if it is paneled. Cut pieces of paper to fit the panels exactly, and paint the rest of the door.

• Use the room's paper on a folding screen.

• Line drawers with wallpaper.

• Brighten the interior of a closet with paper.

• Cut a piece of paper to fit the top of a chest or dresser, put it in place with just a spot or two of adhesive, then cover it with glass.

• Make an old and beatup piece of furniture into an attractive piece by papering ends, tops, drawer fronts. The use of a protective coating for the paper (such as Resistane) will give the paper extra life. Pick a good color from the paper and use it for the drawer dividers, corner posts, and other parts of the furniture that can't be papered easily.

• Make a decorative coup out of a piece of wallpaper, positioned on a plain wall over a sofa, a bed, or another outstanding piece of furniture. Put a molding around it, as though you were framing a picture. On a big wall, "frame" two or three patches. Paint the molding white—or one of the good colors in the paper.

• Wallpaper any plain little box, to make a jewelbox of it, matching the walls of your room.

One method of handling an entire wall as a unit is this combination of background paper and "draperies." Once up, it provides a dramatic setting for a special piece of furniture or a grouping.

• Don't let the bathroom be 100 percent clinical; paper one wall, at least, using one of the modern papers that aren't bothered by water. (Same thing in the kitchen, where a patch of color and pattern over selected countertops where spatter damage is least likely makes the place more pleasant to be in.)

PICKING PAINT COLORS TO GO WITH PAPER. Wallpaper is colorful. That's what you like about it. Most patterns come in a variety of ink colors and background colors.

The most common practice is to paint nonpapered walls, trim, and other nonwall areas of a room the color of the paper background. This practice is perfectly good, and perfectly safe. There may be other ways to pick color schemes that are more interesting without being bizarre or outlandish.

A great many very good wallpapers are done in two colors. For instance there may be a background of very pale green'ochre on which a pattern is printed in a deep oxide red. When your choice is one of these very fine designs, you are held to just two colors: the ochre or the red. Custom color lines in paint stores can match them for you. You'll have a lovely room. It will be a quiet, dignified room if you pick the ochre. It will be a more lively, exciting room if you pick the red.

Take another example. The background is a sunflowery yellow. The major pattern color is a brown-orange. A secondary pattern color is blue. Taking the possibilities in order to their daringness: what or off-white; a yellow to match the background; the brown-orange, to take off on the same level as the most conspicuous pattern color; blue, to support the small amounts of blue in the paper.

Now—how about a one-color paper, such as grasscloth. It is basically brown. It ranges in tiny and subtle shadings from pale tan to deep shoe-leather browns. What colors do you use? There is, to begin with, white—preferably a white that is a little *off*-white on the brown side. There are all the perfectly honorable brown shades. Then, there are all the accent applications, such as blue, green, red. The choice is not simple. Be guided, however, by the promise given you in Chapter 8, on color, that *you* are the best judge in the world of the colors that you like best.

CHAPTER FIFTEEN

THE MATERIALS AND TOOLS OF PAPER HANGING

HANGING PAPER is simple, because the tools and materials involved are simple—easy to use, easy to shop for. A handful of tools and brushes and some makeshift working facilities put you in as good shape as the most professional paper hanger in town. He may have some tools you don't have—but if you did have the tools without his skills and experience, they'd just delay things. Here are some practical ideas to take with you when you shop at the wallpaper store.

PICKING THE PAPER. A wallpaper store may have fifty or a hundred books of patterns. From the standpoint of appearance, you'll surely find what you're looking for. Among other, nonesthetic, considerations are these:

Washability. For an adult bedroom, a living room, a study, it makes little difference whether a wallpaper is washable, since any paper is easy to keep clean except for really dirty dirt. And—there are special liquids for treating papers to make them more washable, which is to say less susceptible to dirtying. But in kitchens, nurseries, and other areas where utility may dictate something less than meticulous care, you should concentrate on those wallpaper books displaying papers labeled "washable." The degree of washability varies upward from papers that are specially treated to prevent their colors from running to papers made with scrubbable plastics such as vinyl.

Hangability. Papers come in several widths—18, 20½, 24, 26, 28 inches, and more. There are several reasons why, the most important of which is freedom of design. Sometimes the designer can turn out a better-looking paper if the pattern is not hampered by a relatively narrow dimension. The narrower papers are easier to hang than wider rolls; there is often less waste with the smaller dimensions when you work around many windows and doors. (Some papers come in sheets—most frequently imported Orientals.)

Some papers are ready-pasted—a tremendous convenience in hanging. However, you may run into trouble with these wallcoverings unless the wall you put them on is in good shape for covering. Many professionals ignore the prepasting, and use regular paste right on top of it. On the other hand, if you are careful, half your work is already done for you when you buy a ready-pasted pattern. It should be possible to satisfy almost any requirement from the lines of a dozen or more producers of papers with the paste already on, although some of the more exotic textures, grasscloth,, burlaps, etc., aren't available in this form.

Also, some papers are ready trimmed. It makes very little sense to buy a paper that isn't. If the pattern you like happens to have the selvage left on, most wallpaper houses have special machines to trim it off. However, not all widths will fit these machines—and it is generally unsatisfactory to run vinyl papers through them, since the pressure of the cutting wheel may delaminate the vinyl and the backing and, in fact, may not cut the tough plastic material cleanly.

HOW MUCH PAPER DO YOU NEED? It has always been one of the mysteries of the wallpaper world that prices, coverage, and other computations are always based on "the single roll"—but they always sell it by the double roll, or more.

No matter what the width of the paper happens to be, a "single roll" of it will cover about 30 square feet of wall. This is the figure to use in computing the number of rolls you must buy. The following chart makes the job of figuring easy:

CEILING HEIGHT	8 Feet	9 Feet	10 Feet	11 Feet	12 Feet		Single Rolls Needed For Ceiling
Size of Room	Single Rolls	Single Rolls	Single Rolls	Single Rolls	Single Rolls	Yards of Border	
8 x 10	9	10	11	12	13	13	3
10 x 10	10	11	13	14	15	15	4
10 x 12	11	12	14	15	16	16	4
10 x 14	12	14	15	16	18	17	5
12 x 12	12	14	15	16	18	17	5
12 x 14	13	15	16	18	19	18	6
12 x 16	14	16	17	19	21	20	6
12 x 18	15	17	19	20	22	21	7
12 x 20	16	18	20	22	24	23	8
14 x 14	14	16	17	19	21	20	7
14 x 16	15	17	19	20	22	21	7
14 x 18	16	18	20	22	24	23	8
14 x 20	17	19	21	23	25	24	9
14 x 22	18	20	22	24	27	25	10
16 x 16	16	18	20	22	24	23	8
16 x 18	17	19	21	23	25	24	9
16 x 20	18	20	22	24	27	25	10
16 x 22	19	21	23	26	28	27	11
16 x 24	20	22	25	27	30	28	12
18 x 18	18	20	22	24	27	25	11
18 x 20	19	21	23	26	28	27	12
18 x 22	20	22	25	27	30	28	12
18 x 24	21	23	26	28	31	29	14

Deduct one single roll for every two windows or doors of average size. Be sure to buy enough, and if there is any doubt, buy an extra roll. This is the only way you can be sure of a perfect match, because if you have to go back later after another roll, there is a chance it may not be exactly the same. The reason for this is that most wallpaper stores cannot carry in stock the fantastic quantities of paper they would need to sell you your needs off their own shelves. You order from a catalog, and the store gets your needs from a central warehouse. Thus, if you order fourteen rolls, and run out, your dealer may find that the exact "run" of paper you bought originally is not available. Wallpaper dealers say that the single greatest complaint from their customers is mismatching of colors between two runs. It cannot always be avoided, except by the purchase, at the beginning, of enough paper. Actually, it is not unwise to have an extra roll of paper tucked away in the attic, anyway, in case some serious sort of damage makes it necessary to put up fresh paper.

If you decide on one of the extra expensive papers or fabrics, particularly those in sheets or other unorthodox forms, you may want to make a scale drawing of the four walls of your room, and figure carefully how you can utilize the paper most advantageously, with the leftover from one special fitting scheduled into another odd-shaped place. It is a fortunate coincidence that some of the highest-priced papers are designed in a way that lets you use practically every inch, without much waste.

Paper for ceilings. You'll notice that the chart for computing the amount of paper you'll need includes a column for ceilings. Is there a reason for papering a ceiling? Very, very rarely, unless you insist on a pattern overhead. In the old days there were special ceiling papers, either plain or very subtle in pattern, and it almost went without saying that you papered the ceiling if you papered the walls. It is, in fact, hard to paper a ceiling. If you have not committed yourself, from the standpoint of appearance, to a ceiling with red, red roses or somesuch on it—paint the ceiling for far less money and with far less work.

TOOLS FOR PAPERING. Wallpapering tools and accessories are simple and inexpensive. You can buy a brush for applying paste for $1—or you can use your paint roller. A smoothing brush can also be in the extra-low-price brackets, although you may want to buy one with synthetic bristles that is easier to keep clean and free of paste. A seam roller and a wheel-type cutter are both in the dollar-or-so class, and so is the "utility knife," if that's what you decide to use. Add to this the price of a plastic pail for paste—or press a kitchen kettle into service.

You need a place to work, cutting, trimming, and pasting the paper. For this, nothing beats a piece of ¾-inch plywood 2 by 8 feet—a standard sheet ripped down the middle at your lumberyard. Put it on two sawhorses, or on the dining-room table, with suitable protection. Next, you must have a straightedge—if your paper is not trimmed. It's hard to find a straighter edge than an uncut side of a piece of ¼-inch plywood. Get a strip about 4 inches wide off one edge of a standard sheet. You can buy

You need a pail, a paste brush, a smoothing brush, a cutter, a seam roller, and some string to be a wallpaper hanger. Everything is cheap to buy, easy to use.

Chemicals are equally uncomplicated: wallpaper remover, wall size, paste, and protective coatings which make paper less likely to get dirty and easier to clean if it does. Some of the auxiliary materials are adhesion improvers, spot dirt removers, and special materials to reduce problems of vermin feeding on the grain-starches of some of the materials. Not all paper stores handle all the products shown, but they surely carry variations of them. Pastes should be adapted to the specific type of paper. There are extra rugged types for heavy cloth and vinyl wallcoverings.

One of the few problems amateur paper hangers find difficult is cutting. Knife-type cutters are generally hard to use, since they tear the paper. Easiest cutters to handle are the wheel type: left, a toothed version which, in a sense, perforates the paper, making it easy to tear true. The simpler knife-edge wheel doesn't cut the paper so much as it scores it—to make tearing easy.

Self-pasted paper has a dried adhesive already spread, needing only to be moistened. All you do is immerse the rolled-up cut strip in a tray of water and let it soak a minute or two—then lift it out—let it drain—and put it on the wall. The tray shown is folded up from prescored heavy waxed cardboard. The bathtub or kitchen sink works as well or better.

Handy though not essential is a combination chalkline and plumb bob, to mark true vertical for hanging the first strip.

To use the self-chalking plum bob, let it hang from a tack at the ceiling until it comes to rest, press the line against the wall without disturbing it laterally, pull it out an inch or two and let it snap. This is called "snapping a line"—perfectly straight and vertical. Avoid too much chalk on the line, or it may show through thin papers.

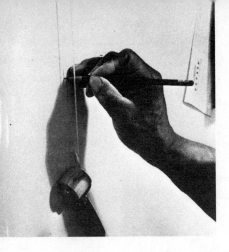

As an alternative, simply hang your seam roller on a length of cord, let it come to a stop vertically, and make several pencil marks along the string.

professional straightedges, with metal guides and other refinements, but they aren't worth it for the amount of paper hanging the average home-owner is likely to do himself. A carpenter's square is handy if you have one, but you can get by without it by lining up paper with the end and the edge of the board to make a square-cut end. And, a pair of scissors.

Materials and supplies. In the order you'll use them, you need some or all of the following: wallpaper remover, wall size, wallpaper paste, paste strengthener, paper conditioner, and paper cleaner. This is what they're for:

• Paper remover is a chemical which helps ordinary water soak wall-paper loose. You need it unless the paper doesn't need to be removed or unless you decide to use a steamer to remove old paper.

• Wall size serves two functions. First, it conditions the wall for best adhesion, making it easier to slip paper into position and have it stay there. Second, it makes it much easier to remove paper when the time comes, since it forms a "release layer" that gives way more readily than paste.

• Wallpaper paste comes in powder and liquid form, and in several grades or strengths. You match the paste to the material you are hanging, using extra-strong stuff for heavy papers, fabrics, vinyls, etc., ordinary paste for lighter coverings. Labels on the containers recommend each paste for its best use. Paste strengtheners are thick liquids to be reduced with water, then added to wallpaper paste to increase its adhesion. They may not be necessary, if you buy the right paste for the job, although you may be able to save a little money with a less sophisticated paste fortified with the strengthener.

• Paper conditioners are materials which reduce the tendency of paper to stain or soil, and make it easier to clean them when they do.

• Paper cleaners come in the form of spray, dough, and various liquids, powderizing dirt lifters, and others. You may find them harder on the dirt and easier on the paper than ordinary soaps.

Instructions for the use of some of these materials is given in the chapter on the specifics of wallpaper hanging.

CHAPTER SIXTEEN

FINAL STEPS BEFORE YOU START

THE VERY capable gentleman in the white overalls who hangs paper for a living can put paper on the wall twice as fast as you can—because he knows how. But if you tried to use all the tricks that speed his work along, you might never get the job done.

You *can* nevertheless, hang paper just as well as he does, using modifications of some of his techniques while imitating him exactly in others. In this chapter you'll find the paper hanging how-to of the home-based handyman, all checked out as workable for the man who doesn't want to make a career of it—who just wants to paper a room or two.

STEPS THAT COME BEFORE THE PAPER GOES UP. The walls you are going to paper fall into one of three classifications, each requiring its own type and degree of preparation:

• Previously papered walls can be repapered if the old paper is on tight—not peeling or lifting—and if there are not too many layers of old paper. Some experts say three layers are too many, others allow four. It depends to a large degree on the kind of paper that was used. Embossed papers, for instance, bulk up more than smooth papers, making an unsolid backing for new wallcoverings. If there is too much paper on the wall, take it off. If the old paper is okay, be sure it is clean and free from oil and grease which might form a poor adhesion base for new paper. (See below for removal techniques.)

If wallpaper is loose only in spots, but tight otherwise, you don't have to take off all the paper. Pull off what comes easily, attempting to leave a gradual torn edge where it is stuck on. If the edge is rough, feather it smooth with sandpaper, or it will show under the new paper.

• Previously painted walls are usually excellent for paper hanging, unless they happen to be painted with a high-gloss enamel. Adhesion may be bad to glossy surfaces. To insure against the whole job coming off the walls, ask your paint dealer for a "deglosser" such as Wil-Bond or Liquid Sandpaper. These materials are strong solvents; be sure to use them with good ventilation. A less expensive method of deglossing the walls is with a saturated solution of trisodium phosphate in hot water. Work with a sponge-mop just wet enough so that it doesn't drip. Rub down the walls until the color of the enamel shows on the surface of the sponge. Rinse well.

Walls painted with ordinary wall paint only need to be clean to form excellent wallpaper base. Beware particularly of oil and grease, which would foil the water-mixed pastes used in paper hanging.

• New walls present no problem if they are plastered and properly aged. If they are plasterboard, *you should give them one good coat of oil-base wall primer before you paper*. It is not necessary to do this in order to do a good initial job of papering. But, if you should ever want to remove the paper from a wall papered over unpainted plasterboard, you might ruin the wall getting the paper off. There is little joy in painting a wall, then putting paper over it. But look forward to the day when you might wish you had.

Plastered walls are alkaline, and until the alkalinity ages away, it may cause stains and color changes in wallpaper. For that reason, proper aging is necessary. Normally, you don't have to worry about this, since scheduling of house building usually calls for plastering far enough ahead of completion so that the alkali problem is gone. However, *if you patch walls* with patching plaster, you may create "hot spots." The easiest way to get rid of them is to brush on a coat of shellac, which seals the hot spots in. Another way is to treat them with acetic acid (see below under "sizing.")

Patching wall damage. The same degree of care in patching cracks in plastered walls is necessary for papering as for painting. Any roughness is visible through the paper, particularly under cross lighting.

Many times a crack in plaster occurs after the previous paper was put on. The result may be merely a line of wrinkles in the paper. If cracks are small you may be able to sand these wrinkles smooth and paper over them without any other repair work. When this light treatment will not suffice, you must tear away the paper and clean the crack of any loose or crumbling material, the same as you would for patching before painting.

Most homeowners find it easiest to patch cracks with a vinyl paste material, available ready to use at paint and paper stores. Its advantages are ease of handling, good adhesion, and no alkalinity. You can paper over it almost immediately. If you use a standard patching plaster, the waiting time is longer for the patch to set and dry, and then it must have a coat of shellac to seal the alkalinity off, or a rather elaborate treatment with acetic acid to neutralize the alkaline characteristic. Nevertheless, when patching is extensive, your vote may be for patching plaster for reasons of economy.

Sometimes an old wall is so badly crazed and cracked that it defies repair by normal methods. However, making it ready for paper is simpler than it would be to prepare it for a decent-looking paint job. Two methods are most frequently used:

• Add about a half pound of plaster of paris to a pound of wall size,

Sizing goes on the wall fast with a roller, makes it easier to hang paper now—easier to take it off when the time comes, years from now. It also locates alkali spots.

mix the dry ingredients, then add the recommended amount of water— usually 11 pints or a little more. The resulting mixture, applied with a large brush, tends to fill small cracks and make the wall smooth enough for papering.

• "Lining paper" is an inexpensive, nonpatterned paper intended for application to bad walls as a smoothing medium. It goes on fast, it bridges most small cracks and crevices, and provides a good base for a regular wallpaper.

How and when to use wall size. Wall size comes in powder or paste form, in paste or in gelatin formulas, for dilutions with water and application by brush or roller. You can control the effectiveness of wall size by the amount of water you put in it, and also by the number of applications. When a wall is absorbent or rough, a slightly thicker mix (less water) is preferred. In extreme cases, use two thin coats. Drying is very rapid. You can go around a room once, then go right around again. Since appearance means nothing, although complete coverage does, wall sizing goes fast.

Although the basic purpose of wall size is to give you a good, uniform surface which paper will *go on and strip loose from* easily, it has another function, less common but invaluable. Most wall sizes contain natural or added "color indicators" which turn purple or pink in the presence of alkali. Thus, they warn you of hot spots of alkali which would ruin your wallpaper. When the wall size dries, you can brush a coat of shellac over the alkali areas—the purple or pink spots. This puts a barrier between the alkali and the paper. Another method—one that is surer not to "leak"— is to bathe the colored areas with a solution of acetic acid. Buy some "28 percent acetic" from your photo supply dealer, if the paint and paper store doesn't have it. Dilute the acid in two parts of water, making it about 7 percent. Swab the acid on the hot spot until the color indicator disappears—indicating in reverse that the alkalinity has been neutralized. Ordinary household vinegar can be used for this neutralization, although it is quite weak and takes longer.

When wall size is dry on the wall, it has a minutely rough or "toothy" feel when you rub your hand over it.That's the best surface for papering.

Important information about calcimine. You cannot paper over calcimine or any of the old-fashioned casein paints. They are not "stuck on the wall" tight enough, themselves, and the paper pulls them off. They must be removed with soap and water. Although this admonition is important, it is not commonly necessary, since very few walls you see these days have anything as primitive on them as calcimine or casein paint. However, in very old houses, which have not been kept up to date, you may encounter the problem. If you think a paint on a wall may be calcimine or casein, give it a swipe or two with good soapy water on a sponge. Does it come off? Then, take it all off.

HOW PAINTING WORKS IN WITH PAPERING. As you read in the chapter on the use of color (Chapter 8), trim and woodwork in papered rooms is usually done in a satin enamel the same color as the background of the paper, as one of the appropriate pattern colors or white. The ceiling, most of the time, is white, off-white, or perhaps one of the colors from the paper background or pattern, preferably a light color, to avoid the feeling of a "glowering" ceiling.

Of course, you paint the ceiling first, and it is most common practice to paint the trim before you paper. If something in your scheduling makes it inconvenient to paint all of the trim first, you should at least take care of baseboards, door and window casings, picture molds, chair rails, and other elements of the woodwork which are adjacent to papered surfaces. The reason for this, of course, is that you do not want to smear paint accidentally on the clean wallpaper. On the other hand, if wallpaper paste happens to get on the enameled woodwork, it is a simple matter to take it off clean with a damp cloth.

It is important to emphasize the proper method of choosing a color for a picture mold, since this vital part of woodwork forms a line between wall and ceiling. Improperly handled, it makes a gauche, disturbing line; properly done the line blends into ceiling and wall and disappears. These are the choices:

- If the ceiling is white, or off-white, make the picture mold the same

Paint all the trim before you start to paper. Make the crown or picture mold the color of the ceiling, or the color of the paper background, regardless of other trim colors, except in special circumstances covered in the text.

color. It is not necessary to switch to an enamel for this. Use the regular ceiling paint.

• If the trim color is the same as the background of the paper, you can make the picture mold that color, too, although this is more difficult, involving the tedious cutting of a color line all around, between the ceiling and the molding. Although a properly installed picture mold is held down a fraction of an inch from the ceiling, this painting is difficult and awkward to reach. You've got to want it pretty badly to paint it another color than the ceiling color to go to all the bother.

• If you select a color from the pattern for the trim, you still must choose between ceiling color and paper background color for the picture mold, unless you *want* the effect of a sharp line around the room at the ceiling.

• In cases where you decide for one reason or another to put the wall pattern on the ceiling, the background color of the paper is the best choice for the picture mold, again unless you are after a completely unorthodox effect, in which case you can go the whole way and enamel the picture mold the best fuchsia or purple-green in the whole pattern.

Most paint stores today have custom-color systems with which they can match any color in any wallpaper, in wall paint or alkyd or latex enamel.

CHAPTER SEVENTEEN

HOW TO MAKE WALLPAPER LOOK ITS BEST

UNLESS YOUR wallpaper is very quiet in tone and pattern, you must think of it somewhat as a "picture" on each wall, framed by the ceiling, the floor, and the two adjacent walls. If there are windows on the wall, too, as there most often are, they must be taken into consideration, as well.

What you must do is compose a picture which looks best, using the paper and the windows, etc., as elements. To do this, think of these three factors:

• The position of the pattern *up and down* on the wall. The point at which the pattern breaks at the ceiling is often critical. It is less so at the floor, since the joint between the floor and the wall is usually covered to a great extent by furniture. Sometimes a paper looks best if the break at the ceiling is right in the *middle* of a pattern. Sometimes it is best if the break is exactly *between* patterns. Mask off the paper with a big sheet of cardboard or newspaper, and decide which looks best to you.

The ceiling line is important for another reason. Very rarely is a house so true and square and plumb that the line where wall and ceiling meet is exactly horizontal. Therefore, if you hang your paper vertically (as you should) and if you match it carefully, strip by strip, you will establish a true horizontal in the pattern. Now, if that horizontal is not matched by horizontality in the ceiling, the difference can be very apparent. For that reason, avoid hitting the ceiling break with a prominent element of the pattern—one that would appear conspicuously to slant up or down. All in all, it is best to put the ceiling break at a fairly neutral point in the pattern, halfway between the repeats in the pattern.

• The position of the pattern laterally makes a difference, too. Many papering instructions tell you to start at one corner. This is fine, if the wall happens to be an even number of roll widths wide. Otherwise, you can end up with an awkwardly narrow strip in the opposite corner.

A better way to do it is to center the pattern from side to side on the wall. When you do this, *either a seam or a strip* will be in the center of the wall, depending on whether it takes an even number or an odd number

Use a trimmed roll to mark off the number of strips a wall will take, in order to determine the best methods of centering the pattern on a wall or around windows, doors, or other features.

Give careful attention to the way a pattern works up to window frames, etc., to achieve the best result. As shown here, the flowers seem to be growing gracefully out from behind the trim. At another point on the pattern, they would seem to be growing awkwardly into the trim.

In prominent situations, such as an outside corner, avoid placing aligned unit of pattern right at the edge. If you do, any lack of plumb, true, and square is more apparent. In this photo, the corner is slightly out of plumb, as a study of the vertical pattern shows. However, it is not readily noticeable, since an inconspicuous part of the pattern follows the edge.

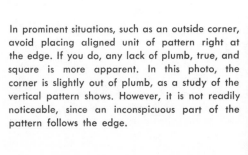

The point in a pattern where it strikes the ceiling is important—much more so than the break at the baseboard. Try to find a place where there is relatively little pattern in random-type figures like this floral. However, when you handle a medallion or other formal pattern, it is usually best to split a unit of pattern in half at the ceiling.

Part of your planning must involve utilizing the pattern break most efficiently. Some patterns run straight across, others "drop." To check out the best way to handle drop patterns, start by sticky-taping one strip on the wall. Then match a strip next to it. There will be surplus at top and bottom. To minimize waste, you may find it best to match alternate strips as you cut them from the roll, rather than to match each strip with the one that you cut last.

This crayon marking on the wallpaper illustrates the principle of the "half drop" paper. The pattern repeats between the upper circle and the lower. On the adjacent strip, however, the same point in the design is only "half a repeat" lower.

to finish the wall. To determine this, take a roll of paper and a pencil, and start in the center of the wall, marking roll widths across the wall into the other corner. If you end up with *less than half* a roll in the corner, you should put a *strip* in the center of the wall. If you end up with *more than half a roll* in the corner, you should put a *seam* in the center of the wall. This way, you center the pattern with uniform strips in each corner the maximum possible width.

• The location of windows on a wall is a third factor in planning the way you should hang the paper. Remember that any straight, hard line which cuts along the pattern of the paper makes a conspicuous joining between plain (the trim) and fancy (the paper). If this hard line is at one point on the pattern on one side of the window and a different point on the other side, and if the pattern is pronounced, it may look like the window is off center or out of position. (It never looks like the paper is misapplied.) This is true, also, of doors.

When a window—or a group of windows—is centered on the wall, the centering of the pattern on the wall takes care of the problem. Fortunately, in most house design, windows *are* centered on walls. But, if you have a wall on which the window is not centered, and if that wall is prominent in the way the room is viewed and lived in, it may be more important to *center the pattern around that window* than to center it on the wall.

When the location of a window off center on a wall makes you decide in favor of centering the pattern on it, instead of on the wall, do it this way:

Find the center of the window—or the grouping of windows. Use a roll to scribe off the number of strips you need to go into the farthest corner. If you end up in the corner with less than half a roll, put a strip in the center of the window or window unit. If you end up with more than half a strip, put a seam in the center. Either way, you put the window in the middle of the pattern break, and you use the widest possible strips on the main part of the wall.

You will not hang wallpaper by this method very long before you discover that it gives you mismatched corners. If you did every wall in the room by the window centering system, you'd have four mismatched corners. That brings up the final step in planning wallpaper for the best appearance.

Rarely does a room have more than two—or three at the most—corners which are critical. By that is meant corners which are unobstructed joinings of two walls . . . corners that you see when you enter the room, or look toward more or less continuously as you sit in the room in normal living. Very often, a doorway in a corner, or a piece of furniture, make it immaterial whether a pattern of the wallpaper matches perfectly or not.

• When a corner is important and conspicuous, make a good pattern match there, regardless of other less important factors.

• When a corner is broken by doorways, shelves, furniture, paneling, or other elements, it can be the place where you let the pattern fall where it will.

Rooms of irregular shape present you with the same prominent-corner decision. If there is an *outside corner* that is hard to overlook, use good judgment in the way you work the pattern around it.

You will find suggestions for making wallpaper look its best in very few instruction manuals, and you will find very few professional paper hangers who will come up with the best arrangement of the patterns vs. corners vs. windows, etc., on their own. That is why a wallpapering job done by a homeowner with tender loving care is often a nicer job than the one done by even the best full-time paper hanger. After all, the mechanics of hanging paper are simple enough, as the next chapter will reveal.

CHAPTER EIGHTEEN

PAPER HANGING STEP BY STEP

FEW THINGS you do around the house are so completely a step-by-step proposition as hanging paper. The entire process is a series of simple steps which must follow one another in the proper sequence for the best, fastest, and easiest job.

1. Cutting the paper into strips. Paper comes in rolls, and must be cut into strips slightly longer than the wall is high. Why not *exactly* as long as the wall is high? Because of a situation called "pattern drop." Most wallpaper patterns are designed so that each strip must be positioned a little lower (or higher) than the preceding one, in order for design elements to continue smoothly from strip to strip. Designers do this so the pattern won't be monotonous, as it would be if there were side-by-side matching, which would put all elements of a pattern in a row across the wall, repeating in every strip. With the "drop" method, the pattern elements do repeat, but only in *every other row*.

To accommodate this factor in design, paper must be cut into strips long enough to reach from ceiling to baseboard *and match*. When patterns are small, the drop may be only an inch or two. When patterns are deliberately symmetrical, such as medallions and some other classic papers, there may be no drop at all. Therefore, you must always work out the method of cutting out the strips which works for *your* wall height and *your* selected pattern. Do it this way:

• Measure the height of the wall, from baseboard to ceiling or picture mold. If you have a long strip of wood around the place, cut it to this exact length, and use it as a handy measuring instrument at all times.

• Unroll a roll of the paper across the floor until a strip the height of the wall plus about 2 feet is exposed.

• Lay out your rule or your measuring stick on the paper so that one end is even with the best cut-off point for the ceiling (see Chapter 17) and there is a surplus of paper at the other end—a couple of inches is enough.

• Cut off the strip. Then, pull the roll down and unroll another strip *beside* the first one. Adjust this strip, before you cut it, so that the pattern matches at the edges. Cut it off at the bottom, as before, with a couple of inches extra, and at the top, even with the first strip. *Important:* If your house is fairly new and fairly true, you can cut the tops square, and plan on positioning them right at the ceiling as you hang; otherwise, let them be an inch or two long at the top, to allow for ups and downs and uneven walls.

Depending on the exact dimension of your walls and the exact size of the pattern, you may find that matching the drops results in very little waste. If, however, you find that the waste is sizable, experiment with these ideas, in search of a more efficient utilization of paper:

Try matching *every other* strip in the roll.

Try matching one strip on one side, the next on the other.

Try working off two rolls, alternately.

Be sure to keep strips in order, so you can handle them without losing the match. It's a good idea to make a pile of them and roll them up in a tight roll in the opposite curl from the original. This will take some of the fight out of the paper and make it easier to work with.

2. Pasting the paper. Professionals put the paste on the paper in a way that is neat and tidy—for them—and often messy for amateurs.

They place the pile of strips face down on the pasting table. They pull the top strip to the front edge of the table, and let it hang over about a quarter-inch. The top of the paper goes a quarter-inch over one end of the table. With the paper in this position, they brush on paste over about half of the strip. Since one edge of the paper hangs over the table— as does one end—and the other edge is on the back of the next strip, they slop paste over nothing that makes any difference; the next strip is going to be pasted soon, anyway.

With half the strip pasted, the professionals fold the pasted part over itself, and brush on the other half. Then they fold this half over. In a few moments the paper is "cured" and ready to go up.

You can work this way if you want to, and with a little practice you'll get good at it. At first, however, you'll get a lot of paste where you don't want it, and the next sheet in line will get badly "over-cured" where you slopped paste on it.

It is usually best for the once-a-year-or-less paper hanger to work one sheet at a time. Cover your paste table (ideally a 2-by-8 sheet of ¾-inch plywood) with many thicknesses of newspaper. Lay out a strip. Paste it. Remove the messy layer of newspaper and you're ready for the next sheet. Nevertheless, some of the professional's tricks belong in your bag.

• Don't mix the paste too thin. Many instructions on the paste labels recommend a certain quantity of water for "light" papers and a lesser amount for "heavy" papers. It's best always to use a little less water than recommended as the leanest mixture. It gives you better, more certain adhesion, it makes the paper slip into place more readily, and it compensates for a little unevenness in paste application.

• Be sure to put plenty of paste on the paper. Don't brush it out thin. If you use a roller—one of the good ideas—dip the roller often and don't spread it too much. Work for uniformity in application.

• Fold the top quarter down and the bottom quarter up, as the professional does. This is a critical step. First, it helps make the spread of paste uniform, because the two pasted surfaces come together and share their loads. Second, it puts the paper in a position to avoid the evaporation of water from the glue while the paper cures.

• Give a pasted and folded strip up to 10 minutes to cure. By curing is meant, merely, a chance to let the paste permeate the paper, softening it for easiest handling. Not every wall is perfectly flat and true, and you must sometimes stretch the paper a little here and there. Cured, the paper stretches readily. Curing also promotes uniformity of paper wetting within each strip and from strip to strip, so matching is easier and better.

Once you get into the swing of things, you may want to paste a strip, lay it aside while you paste another, then hang the first one and paste the third, while the second is curing. This rotation soon gets into a routine that gives you uniformly cured and easily hung paper.

3. Put the paper on the wall. Before the first strip goes up, you must determine absolute vertical—so you won't hang the paper crooked. Use a regular plumb bob, or improvise one as shown in the photographs. If you snap a line, don't use too much of a chalk that is too dark, or it may show through the paper. Where you snap the line or mark the vertical depends on how you are balancing the paper on the wall (see Chapter 17), since it will be most effective if you hang a full strip to the vertical marking.

• Unfold the top of the paper, and holding it by the corners, raise it into position at the ceiling. Try not to let it swing against the wall until you have it in position. Then, touch the paper to the wall at the top. Hold it away lower down until you swing it laterally to match up with the vertical line-up.

• Gently push the paper against the wall, and give it a swipe with the smoothing brush, to hold it. Do not brush hard yet. Do not brush all over yet.

• Step back and take a look. When you are satisfied as to position, verticality, and line-up at the ceiling, brush down the top half of the paper.

• Now unfold the bottom half. Hold it away from the wall, and gradually bring it into contact with a downward sweep of the smoothing brush.

At this point, the strip of paper is on the wall. Check it carefully for position, then smooth and firm it with the smoothing brush. The best way to do this is with a three-stroke series. Bring the brush down the middle of the paper—or stroke it upward. Then stroke from the middle to the edges, in both directions.

The second strip goes up in the same way, except that you must position it carefully for match—and for joint. At this point, you'll have your first experience *sliding* the paper up against the preceding strip. You carry the strip to the wall in the same manner as the first.

An efficient setup for wallpapering is a 2-by-8-foot piece of ¾-inch plywood placed on a dining room or kitchen table.

To cut top ends of strips square, use either of these methods: Line up the edge of the paper with the edge of your plywood working table, then crease it over the end (top). This gives you a square crease-line to cut on with scissors. Or, use a carpenter's square, carefully lined up as a tearing edge (bottom).

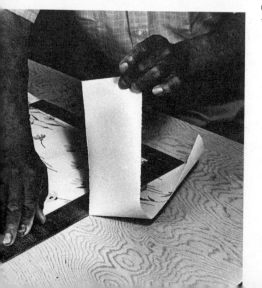

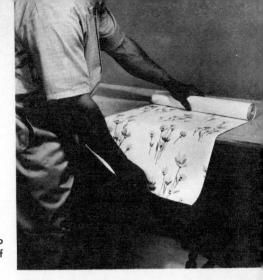

The paper always curls coming off the roll. To make it lie flat, draw it gently over the edge of the table.

If your paper is not trimmed, use a strip off the edge of a sheet of plywood or masonite as a straightedge, and a utility knife. Cut the paper while it is dry. Many professionals cut untrimmed paper in a different manner, but the utility knife technique is easiest for most amateurs.

The trick, applying paste, is to avoid messing up the work table. One way, shown here, is to pile your paper more or less in the center of the table, then slide the top sheet to one edge, letting it overhang slightly. Extra paste falls on the next sheet to be pasted.

An easier way for most amateurs is to load the table with plenty of newspapers, removing those on top as they get paste on them. Fastest paste spreading is with a roller—but you must be careful not to roll the paste too thin.

When one half of the strip is pasted, lift the end and fold the pasted half over itself. Then do the other half.

Fold the second half over itself, then allow five or more minutes for the paper to "cure"—or gain a uniform dampening throughout.

Be sure to wipe any paste off the face of the paper, after you have pasted it. Keep an eye on the surface as you hang each strip and wipe paste before it has a chance to dry.

When the paper has cured, unfold the top half and carry it to the wall by the corners. Position the paper at the top, holding it away as well as possible farther down the wall. When the position is correct, stroke the paper against the wall with the smoothing brush. The first stroke of the brush should be down the middle of the strip.

Follow with brush strokes to alternate edges of the paper, firming it against the wall.

As you carry succeeding strips to the wall, slide them up to butt against the last one. Firm strokes toward the previous strip gradually work it close. Lift the paper as shown here, as it is difficult to slide, then smooth it down again.

If you do not precut all strips for the ceiling line, follow this technique, cutting them in place. Brush and smooth the paper upward, tapping it into the corner with the bristle ends. Then run the cutter back and forth in the angle two or three times. Pull the paper loose slightly in the angle and again tap with the brush—an action which should break-tear the paper. Use scissors if necessary to make a smooth cut.

Now unfold the bottom half of the paper, smooth it against the wall and work it tight to its neighbor. Pound it in at the baseboard, then use the cutter to trim off the end.

Remove switch and outlet plates, then simply paper over them. When the strip is up, tear away the extra paper.

Working around window sills and other places requires careful work with a scissors.

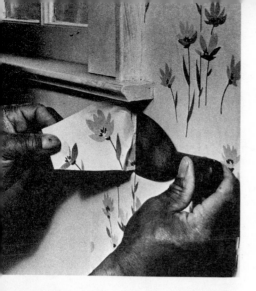

For good clean tears along edges too small to roller-cut, use a putty knife to hold the paper while you make the tear.

After the paste has dried a while—just how long depends on many factors—run the seam roller firmly down the joints in the paper. If paste is squeezed out, wait longer. After a few strips, you'll find out just how long you must delay rolling for the best job.

The last step—when the paper has dried—is application of a paper conditioner to make it more dirt-resistant, and easier to clean when it does get dirty.

- Position the strip at the ceiling, just as you did the first, then check at the key match points, sliding the paper up or down as required to make the proper match.

- At the same time, slide the paper up to the preceding strip, so that the edges come snugly together. Normally, this lateral sliding can be done by brushing with firm strokes in the direction you want the paper to move. If necessary, place the palms of your hands on the paper near the edge and exert pressure sidewise. Your hands should be clean, of course, but if they are slightly damp the extra friction helps.

- If you find you cannot slide the paper up to make a butt with the previous strip, pull it away from the wall and smooth it back down with a lateral motion. You may have to loosen the paper in this manner at the top, then at the bottom, to make the proper joint. *Remember:* You can pull the paper away from the wall, then smooth it back down a great number of times without ruining adhesion, so be patient.

The different kinds of joints. Three different kinds of joints are used in paper hanging. First, there is the ordinary *lap joint,* in which the paper is trimmed on one side only; the other side goes on selvage and all. Ensuing strips cover this edge. Lap joints are not much used in fine papering. Second, there is the *wire edge,* which utilizes trimmed paper, with a lap of only 1/16 or 1/8 of an inch. This makes a somewhat better-looking job, particularly if you use plenty of pressure on the seam roller (see below). The third joint is the *butt joint,* most often used and best looking of all. Making it, you use trimmed paper and there is no lap at all. The butt must be tight, and the seam roller must be used at the proper time. If you buy ready-trimmed paper you are limited to butt joints and wire edges; if you trim it yourself, you can go for the lap joint, if you wish.

4. Trim the ends. As has been suggested, when the wall and ceiling are true, you can precut the top of each strip so that it slides into ceiling or picture mold or crown mold, with no further attention. However, when the ceiling tends to wander somewhat, this is the way to make a clean, snug fit:

- Run the wheel cutter along the ceiling line or the bottom edge of the molding. Make several passes, to score the paper well—or even cut through it if the paper is soft.

- Pull the paper away from the wall, and either tear along the cutter-mark, or cut it smooth with shears. The tear is fastest and it is often best looking, since the slightly feather edge of the torn paper is softer.

- Then, smooth the paper back up into place, with the smoothing brush. Tap it at the top with the ends of the bristles, to firm it down.

The same technique works at the baseboard. Score, pull free, then tear or cut. Sometimes if you pull the paper free not more than a half-inch or so, you can tap along the score mark with the end of the smoothing brush bristles and break the paper at the same time you smooth it back to the wall.

What to do about irregular shapes. In the foregoing step-by-step method, the problem has been straightaway paper hanging. When you come to a window or other obstruction, the best technique is to cut the paper to fit *after it is partially up*—rather than make any sort of an attempt to cut it on the paste table.

Paste the paper in the ordinary manner and give it the standard amount of curing time. Carry it to the wall in the same way as you would on a flat area. Position the paper at the ceiling level, make adjustments for a perfect match, and slide the paper over to make the proper joint. With the smoothing brush, work the paper up snug to the wall and into the corner formed by the window trim and the wall. Now follow these steps:

• Put your finger on the wallpaper at the exact point where it covers a corner of the trim.

• Make a diagonal scissors cut to that point from the edge of the paper over the window.

• Use the smoothing brush to tap the paper into the corner of the wall and trim at the side and across the top.

• At this point, the paper will stick out above and at one side of the window. Use the cutting technique that works best for you at ceilings and baseboards to get rid of this surplus. *Note:* Wallpaper stores sell cutting gadgets of various kinds which may be of help to you in fitting paper. Before you buy one that costs very much, however, remember that very few *slicing,* blade-type cutters will work on wet paper, no matter how well they cut dry paper. When paper is wet and soft, the blade tears it more often than not.

Below the window you find a more complicated situation, but it is handled in the same way as the upper corner. With a series of scissors cuts (see photographs) and edge tearing, you work your way around the end of the sill and the "apron" beneath it.

There is a time when this method of fitting is not feasible: when the space between the last strip and the obstruction is only a few inches and it would not provide enough support for the paper while you did your fitting. In situations such as this, a good method is to cut the paper horizontally at a point just below the top of the window. Paste it over the window, make the diagonal cut, and let the piece come down beside the window a short distance. Now cut an edge from the same strip of paper long enough to come down to the bottom of the apron. The strip should be slightly wider than the space to be filled. Hang this strip, fitting it below the window as described above. Then, with the remaining piece of full-width paper, finish below the window.

This technique leaves you with two horizontal joints in the paper (one at the top, one below) but when the strip is narrow, these joints are hard to detect.

5. Roll the seams. This operation takes place after the paste has started to dry. Its purpose is to force the paper into tight contact with the wall right at the seams, to guard against adhesion failure there—

where it would be most serious. The exact amount of time you should give the paste to dry properly for rolling depends on the amount of paste, the nature of the wall, the humidity in the room, and other factors. There is a rule of thumb, however:

Run the roller down the seams. If paste is forced out, it is too soon. At the point when the paper is still slightly damp but no paste comes through the seam when you roll, everything is exactly right, and experimentation will tell. Eventually, you'll work out a formula, such as "roll the seam of the fourth strip back," that works right for you and your methods.

6. Sponge off paste smears. As you go along, wipe paste smears off the surface of the paper, trim, moldings, etc. If the paper you are using is washable—even mildly so—it won't hurt to dry-sponge the entire surface, to make sure you haven't left unsuspected specks of paste here and there. After you roll the seams, if any paste comes to the surface, be sure to wipe it off.

Wiping with a sponge or damp cloth will usually keep your smoothing brush clean, although you may have to take it to the kitchen sink for a good washing now and then. Shake it and wipe it as dry as possible. Dirt accumulates on roller and cutting knife, too, and must be cleaned away now and then.

THE ORDER OF HANGING, STRIP BY STRIP. As was made clear in Chapter 17, you just can't start hanging paper in one corner of the room and hang willy nilly around the walls till you get back to that corner. For the best looks, you *plan* the entire room—almost wall by wall. And, you must hang the paper to follow the plan. Since this means, basically, centering the pattern on walls or on other predominant features, and since you must put either a seam or a strip in the center, there are two ways to proceed, strip by strip:

1. You can establish the center, determine whether a seam or a strip goes there, and then start hanging paper at the center. If you do this, you hang succeeding strips first on the right, then on the left, gradually working into the corners. Finally, you cut two strips the proper width for the corners. This technique flies somewhat in the face of an old belief that you must keep hanging paste-wet paper next to paste-wet paper, or the shrinkage difference may cause mismatching. Actually, by alternating, you get back soon enough each time with the matching strip so that the wet-to-wet principle still applies; moreover, today's papers have far greater dimensional stability than the softer unfortified papers of years ago.

2. An alternate method, workable in some conditions, is to measure and mark carefully where each seam will fall, starting at the center. Then, with the width of the corner strip carefully established, cut it, hang it, and progress across the wall to the other narrower strip in the other corner.

You must arrange the pile of cut strips in the proper sequence to accommodate whichever of these methods you select.

WHAT TO DO ABOUT ODD SHAPES. Not every wall is rectangular. Sometimes slanting ceilings close under the roof, or dormers, or other architectural features give walls odd shapes and sometimes even result in some questions as to whether an area is wall *or* ceiling.

When a ceiling slants, as often happens in upstairs bedrooms, you'll find it easiest to treat it as ceiling and paint it. The result is attractive, too, unless there is too much ceiling, or the slant is too steep. Suppose in an attic bedroom, or the typical second-story bedroom in a small house, the ceiling slants down to within about 3 or 4 feet of the floor. It wouldn't look right to paint this much area descending into territory normally considered wall. Again, suppose the house design is Dutch Colonial or other style with a gambrel roof which results in what might better be called a "slanting wall" than a slanting roof. It, too, would be better papered.

However, when the roof happens to cut off only a relatively small corner at the ceiling, the appearance is usually best when that small slanting area is painted with the ceiling.

Whenever paper hung vertically on a normal wall meets paper hung on a "slanting wall" or ceiling, match is impossible, of course. Sometimes the line where the two reaches of paper meet is so awkward that you must modify it by nailing up a picture molding, painted the color of the paper background.

The side-walls of dormers, large or small, look best papered, with the ceiling areas painted to match the main part of the room. Of course, the meeting of dormer paper with wallpaper where the two join, forming a slanting outside corner, is a mismatch, the same as the inside corner of a slanting ceiling and its adjacent wall. However, it rarely seems as awkward as the inside corner. In both cases, be sure to carry the paper around the corner in one direction, then cut the proper angle in the paper from the other side and hang it so that the seam falls just short of the corner.

HOW TO CLEAN WALLPAPER. Hopefully, it won't come up for a long time after you hang the paper, but eventually it will need cleaning. How you do it depends on the water-resistance of the paper. Vinyl-coated papers and some other highly waterproof materials withstand pretty vigorous scrubbing. Others may not. To find out the degree of washability of the paper on your wall, pick a spot back of a sofa or some other place that is always covered, and experiment. First, try water, then water with soap or detergent, then detergent and rubbing. Soon you'll find out how much cleaning abuse the paper will stand—but always clean it with the gentlest method that will remove the dirt.

There are many wallpaper cleaners, spot-cleaners, dry-cleaners, "erasers," and so forth on the market. Try them, to see if there might be one that makes the job easiest for you.

Regardless, there is a final step in any paper hanging job that makes the future life of the paper and happiness of the homeowner more secure: a coating of paper conditioner, such as Resistane, which is easy to brush or roll on, easy to keep clean.

INDEX